Lifting
up the
Downcast

Lifting up the Downcast

Patrick Sookhdeo

Isaac Publishing

Lifting up the Downcast

First edition, 2021

Published in the United States of America by
Isaac Publishing
1934 Old Gallows Road, Suite 350
Vienna, VA 22182

Library of Congress Control Number: 2021901169
ISBN: 978-1-952450-06-8

Printed in the United Kingdom

Contents

1

Introduction: the God of peace, hope and love

Why, my soul, are you downcast?
Why so disturbed within me?
Put your hope in God,
for I will yet praise him,
my Saviour and my God.

(Psalm 42:11)

In 1648, Rev. William Bridge preached 13 sermons at Stepney in London, all on the text Psalm 42:11.[1] England was in agony. A bitter and bloody civil war, dividing family members against each other, had raged for six years, and soon (January 1649) would result in the execution the king, causing shock waves of horror. The deadly religious conflicts and persecution of the previous century still reverberated. Extremes of weather caused great hardship, especially for the poor. The summer of

1648 was described as "worse than some of the past winters". The following winter was so cold that London's River Thames froze over. Outbreaks of plague were becoming increasingly common in England and other countries of north-west Europe. Central Europe had been at war for 30 years, originally over religious issues in Germany, with at least 4.5 million deaths, mainly from disease and hunger.

In the midst of this mayhem and danger, people yearned for hope, comfort, solace and stability. No doubt their circumstances weighed heavily on their minds, as we know from our experience of the uncertainties, trials and perils of our own age. As David observed in another psalm, it was as if the foundations were being destroyed; what then should the righteous do, facing an unknown future from which all the old familiar and dependable certainties had been removed? (Psalm 11:3)

A century after William Bridge's set of sermons, a destructive earthquake shook London on 8 March 1750, the worst in what was later called the "year of earthquakes". It was interpreted by most people at the time as a warning or judgment from God. Afterwards John and Charles Wesley published a pamphlet of hymns about the earthquake,[2] including one, which deserves to be better known, beginning:

> From whence these dire portents around,
> That strike us with unwonted fear?
> Why do these earthquakes rock the ground,
> And threaten our destruction near?
> Ye prophets smooth, the cause explain,
> And lull us to repose again.

Perhaps remembering the destruction of the foundations in Psalm 11, as well as Elijah's meeting with the Lord (1 Kings 19:11-12), the last three verses of the hymn run:

> The pillars of the earth are Thine,
> And Thou hast set the world thereon;
> They at Thy threatening look incline,
> The centre trembles at Thy frown;
> The everlasting mountains bow,
> And God is in the earthquake now!

> Now, Lord, to shake our guilty land,
> Thou dost in indignation rise;
> We see, we see Thy lifted hand
> Made bare a nation to chastise,
> Whom neither plagues nor mercies move
> To fear Thy wrath or court Thy love.

> Therefore the earth beneath us reels,
> And staggers like our drunken men,
> The earth the mournful cause reveals,
> And groans our burden to sustain;
> Ordained our evils to deplore,
> And fall with us to rise no more.

Now, and at many times in the past, God's people are experiencing great hardship and hazard, surrounded by calamitous events beyond their control, and facing a daunting future. But He has blessed us with many promises of His peace, with many assurances of certain hope, and with many tokens of His unwavering love. We can build up our faith, as we hold on to His peace, hope and love.

This hymn by John Newton (1725-1807) blends themes of joy, hope, faith, love, strength and overcoming. John Newton's mother was a devout believer who filled her little boy's mind with Scripture. Sadly, she died when he was seven. At the age of eleven, John went to sea with his father, and before long was leading a wild and tumultuous life. At the age of 23, he repented and turned to the Lord, although continuing to captain a slave-trading ship for another six years. Eventually he became an ordained minister and wrote many wonderful hymns. This one is about a believer whose "life is now hidden with Christ in God" (Colossians 3:3 see verse 2 of the hymn), and reminds us that with Jesus to help, strengthen, guide and defend us we can have nothing to fear.

Rejoice, believer, in the Lord

Rejoice, believer, in the Lord,
Who makes your cause His own;
The hope that's built upon His Word
Can ne'er be overthrown.

Though many foes beset your road,
And feeble is your arm,
Your life is hid with Christ in God,
Beyond the reach of harm.

Though many foes beset your road,
And feeble is your arm,
Your life is hid with Christ in God,
Beyond the reach of harm.

Weak as you are, you shall not faint,
Or fainting, shall not die;
Jesus, the strength of every saint,
Will aid you from on high.

Though sometimes unperceived by sense,
Faith sees Him always near,
A guide, a glory, a defence:
Then what have you to fear?

As surely as He overcame,
And triumphed once for you,
So surely you that love His name
Shall triumph in Him too.

John Newton, 1779

The multi-faceted peace of God

Psalm 42 speaks of the soul being bowed down by the weight of a heavy burden and tossed around as if in a boat on a rough sea. If we include Psalm 43 with Psalm 42 – and there is evidence to suggest they were originally a single psalm – the psalmist asks himself six times why he is feeling like this. The very fact that the psalmist keeps questioning why his soul is in this state indicates that it is not the norm for a believer. Inward peace and quietness of soul are characteristic of a Christian. "Our hearts are restless until they find their rest in You," wrote Augustine of Hippo (354-430).[3] However, from time to time this peace can be interrupted and God's people may become discouraged, downcast and disquieted.

The Hebrew word translated "peace" in the Old Testament is *shalom*, meaning wholeness. The uncut stones from which Joshua built an altar on Mount Ebal were literally "*shalom* stones" (Joshua 8:31). The Bible tells us that the rebuilt wall of Jerusalem was "completed" on a certain date. The Hebrew text says that the wall had been "*shalom*-ed" on that date (Nehemiah 6:15). So peace in the Old Testament signifies far more than just a feeling of tranquillity: it means complete well-being of body, mind and spirit. It is interesting to see how this sense is reflected in Paul's prayer for the Thessalonians that the God of peace would sanctify them through and through, and that their "whole spirit, soul and body" be kept blameless at the coming of our Lord Jesus Christ. (1 Thessalonians 5:23).

"Peace" in the New Testament is the Greek word *eirene*, which appears in every book except John's first letter. Its everyday meanings include harmonious relationships between people and between nations, security and lack of conflict, and orderliness. Its specially Christian meanings focus on a harmonious relationship between God and humans, and the sense of rest and contentment which stems from this.

Old and New Testament together tell us that the God of peace (Hebrews 13:20) and His Son the Prince of Peace (Isaiah 9:6) have each promised us peace (Isaiah 57:19; John 14:27). The Holy Spirit also gives us peace (Galatians 5:22).

> The LORD blesses his people with peace.
> (Psalm 29:11)

There are countless assurances in Scripture like this, from which many hymn-writers have written inspirational descriptions of Christian peace.

> Drop thy still dews of quietness
> Till all our strivings cease,
> Take from our souls the strain and stress,
> And let our ordered lives confess
> The beauty of Thy peace.[4]

What if we do not *feel* peace?

Some may say that they do not experience the reality of these promises, that they have put their faith in Christ, they regularly ask Him to forgive their sins, yet they feel troubled and distressed. This is true for many of us at different times in our lives and some of the interruptions to our conscious peace can last a long and weary time. But perhaps we have more peace than we realise. Even when we do not *feel* at peace, it remains the fact that "we have been justified through faith, we have peace with God through our Lord Jesus Christ" (Romans 5:1). The fundamental saving peace of being reconciled to God can never be taken away from us, no matter what is going on in our mind or emotions.

We should remember, also, that peace and joy are different things. We may lack joy but still have peace, like daylight when the sun is behind the clouds. We must remember also to compare our inner state now with what it might have been if we had not put our faith in the Lord. We do not yet have perfect wholeness and peace of mind, but we surely have more than if we were not walking daily with our Saviour.

Is there anything we can do to help restore our peace and wholeness when it has been interrupted? One thing that can be very helpful is to

> Count your blessings, name them one by one;
> Count your blessings, see what God hath done;
> Count your blessings, name them one by one,
> And it will surprise you what the Lord hath done.[5]

The old hymn advises us to do this when we are tossed about in life's storms, "burdened with a load of care", discouraged, perhaps even despairing "thinking all is lost". Likewise William Bridge urged his troubled listeners, in the turmoil of 1648, to make sure they appreciated every morsel that the Lord gave them. He told them to value and treasure it as a love-gift from God, and to use it well, so as to strengthen their faith and increase their inner peace.

> Praise God for every smile, and rejoice in the
> least. If a bowed [i.e. bent] sixpence, as it were,
> be sent you from heaven, lay it up, even every
> love-token. Peace is a tender thing. Does the
> Lord begin to speak peace to any of your souls?

> Now stir up ourselves in a way of believing, and
> then Christ will give you more.[6]

We cannot understand why some receive this felt peace quickly and easily, while others wrestle for a long time before they become conscious of an abiding serenity. But we must remember the parable of the workers in the vineyard who all received the same wages, though some had worked all day and others only for an hour. That was the decision of the owner of the vineyard (Matthew 20:1-15). So let us be thankful for whatever measure of peace the Lord has given us and not compare ourselves with others.

We shall not be perfect until we see the Lord face to face (1 John 3:2; 1 Corinthians 13:9-12). Until then, we are in the process of being transformed into His image with ever-increasing glory (2 Corinthians 3:18). We are a "work in progress", as we grow in holiness (2 Corinthians 7:1; Philippians 1:4-6; Hebrews 10:14). God is building us, as Nehemiah's team built the wall of Jerusalem, and the last stone only goes in place when we reach heaven. That is when we shall be fully "*shalom*-ed". So let us not be too hard on ourselves if our peace is patchy and imperfect now. For we are not yet in that place which the writer to the Hebrews called God's "rest" (Hebrews 4:1). "Soon and very soon, we are going to see the King"[7] and then, when the struggles of this world are left behind for ever, we shall have perfect peace and wholeness.

As committed believers, eager to grow in Christ-likeness, holiness and Christian maturity, and longing to bring joy to our beloved Lord, we may be distressed by our own shortcomings and sins. This is a disturbance to our tranquillity that we have to expect and accept.

"Jesus, my All-in-all Thou art" writes Charles Wesley in verse 3 of this hymn, and from beginning to end his emotion comes pouring out, as Wesley tries to express all that the Lord Jesus means to a Christian, in a rich and glorious cascade of words and images. Some are familiar to every reader of the Bible and some are perhaps unique – "my smile beneath the tyrant's frown".

Thou hidden source of calm repose

Thou hidden source of calm repose,
Thou all-sufficient love divine;
My help and refuge from my foes,
Secure I am if Thou art mine;
And lo! From sin, and grief, and shame,
I hide me, Jesus, in Thy name.

Thy mighty name salvation is,
And keeps my happy soul above;

Comfort it brings, and power, and peace,
And joy, and everlasting love;
To me, with Thy dear name, are given
Pardon, and holiness and Heaven.

Jesus, my All-in-all Thou art –
My rest in toil, my ease in pain,
The medicine of my broken heart,
In war my peace, in loss my gain;
My smile beneath the tyrant's frown;
In shame, my glory and my crown;

In want, my plentiful supply;
In weakness, my almighty power;
In bonds, my perfect liberty;
My light in Satan's darkest hour;
My help and stay whene'er I call'
My life in death, my heaven, my all.

Charles Wesley, 1749

We should also remember that there is a kind of "peace" that is a very un-Christian peace. This is the relaxed and contented attitude of the godless person who is unbothered by their sinful lifestyle and their lack of a relationship with God. This is not a peace that we should seek, envy or yearn for.

True peace is a gift from God. The Bible calls it the peace of God (Philippians 4:7) or the peace of Christ (Colossians 3:15). "My peace," said Jesus, was what He was giving us (John 14:27) and, "I have told you these things, so that in me you may have peace." (John 16:33). He means us to experience this peace whatever our situation, for, He says, "In this world you will have trouble." His peace is not like the peace of the world (John 14:27), that is, a peace due to peaceful circumstances. The peace of God is beyond human understanding (Philippians 4:7).

The peace that we have with God, which Jesus won for us on the cross, should be reflected in our relationships with others. Christians should live in peace with each other (Mark 9:50; 1 Thessalonians 5:13) for Christ Himself is our peace (Ephesians 2:14-17). As far as possible we should with live in peace with everyone (Romans 12:18); in fact we should be active peacemakers (Matthew 5:9).

Confident Christian hope

Closely linked to the gift of peace is the gift of hope. If hope is defined as the joyful expectation of good things to come, then *Christian* hope is the *confident* and joyful expectation of good things to come. Our hope rests on the promises of the God of hope (Romans 15:13) and therefore what we look forward to is certain to come about.

> Let us hold unswervingly to the hope we profess,
> for he who promised is faithful. (Hebrews 10:23)

There are three aspects to Christian hope. Firstly, it should fill the lives of Christ's disciples, just as peace does. We can lean daily on the promises in the Word of God, whether for us as individuals, for God's people as a whole, or for all creation. So we need not give way to despair for ourselves or those we love, for situations we are entangled in or situations we observe from outside.

This world is in the hands of God, who is working out His purposes, and His ways are higher than our ways. Catastrophes and disasters that may seem to a materialistic and atheistic society purely negative can be used by God to draw people back to Himself in repentance and faith. A habit of trustfully seeking God's wisdom and perspective gives us not only hope but also peace and joy, even in the midst of chaos (Romans 15:13). We wear "a garment of praise instead of a spirit of despair" (Isaiah 61:3). That is why the psalmist, determined to lift himself up from his spiritual depression, says to his soul:

> Put your hope in God,
> for I will yet praise him,
> my Saviour and my God.
> (Psalm 42:11)

The second aspect of Christian hope is that, as redeemed sinners, we have a sure and certain hope of heaven when we die (see chapter 5). This hope makes us pilgrim people, for we realise that we are no longer of the world (John 17:13-16), but merely passing through it. We are temporary residents here, and we do not really belong: our permanent citizenship is in heaven (Philippians 3:20). Hope is the first main theme of Peter's letter to persecuted Christians, whom he addresses as scattered exiles, pilgrims, or strangers in the world (1 Peter 1:1-3 NIV, NKJV,

KJV). This hope changes our values, for our treasure is in heaven and our hearts are already there too (Matthew 6:19-21). It affects how we choose to use our short time here on earth.

The third aspect of Christian hope is the Second Coming of our Lord Jesus Christ. Although we cannot know *when* this will happen, we can be sure that it *will* happen, and we must be prepared and ready. Therefore, this too is a hope which affects how we live.

> ... we know that when Christ appears, we shall be like him, for we shall see him as he is. All who have this hope in him purify themselves, just as he is pure.
> (1 John 3:2-3)

Hope gives us strength and courage, so hope is a source of comfort (in the old and Biblical meaning of that wonderful word – see chapter 6).

> Be strong and take heart,
> all you who hope in the Lord.
> (Psalm 31:24)

Hope enables us to be "valiant and steadfast", in the words of the Dutch theologian Brakel, who, writing in a time of persecution, encouraged faithful believers to stand firm and be ready for martyrdom if necessary.[8]

Hope gives us endurance. Paul wrote to the Thessalonian Christians about their "endurance inspired by hope in our Lord Jesus Christ" (1 Thessalonians 1:3). As William Edwy Vine has said, hope "finds its expression in endurance under trial, which is the effect of waiting for the Coming of Christ."[9]

The perfect love of the God of love

Our God is not only the God of peace and the God of hope, but also the God of love (2 Corinthians 13:11). John tells us that God is love (1 John 4:8) and we marvel at the nature of His love, for when we were still sinners Christ died for us to make us children of His heavenly Father (1 John 3:1; Romans 5:8).

For he tells us that perfect love drives out fear (1 John 4:18). Whose is that perfect love? It is surely not ours, for, just as we will not have perfect peace this side of heaven, neither we will have perfect love in this life. The perfect love is the love of God for us, and the fear that it banishes is our fear, as we are filled with peace and hope.

Our Father in heaven, the omnipotent Creator, knows our every need, He loves us with an everlasting love (Jeremiah 31:3), and He provides for us here and in the hereafter. He has already given His Son to die to take away our sins, in order we need have no fear of the next life, so how will He not also graciously give us all the things that we need in this life? (Romans 8:32) Even an earthly father gives good gifts to his children, how much more our heavenly Father (Matthew 7:9-12).

The evil one may be roaming around the world looking for people to devour, but we do not need to be afraid. Jesus has already defeated him on the cross and our Father in heaven laughs at his puny efforts (Psalm 2:4; 37:13). This is the King of kings and Lord of lords, the Lord God Almighty, who made us His children, who knows and loves each one of us, cares about even the smallest things in our lives and can meet even the greatest needs we have. It is His love that gives us peace and hope, and leaves no room for fear or anxiety. (See chapters 2 and 3.)

There is nothing to fear as we rest in God's love.

But there is something to do.

While we enjoy peace, hope, joy, comfort and the other blessings that He lovingly lavishes on us, He calls us to show that same love to each other. Paul urges us:

> Follow God's example, therefore, as dearly loved children and live a life of love, just as Christ loved us and gave himself up for us as a fragrant offering and sacrifice to God.
>
> (Ephesians 5:1-2)

John explains that loving God's other children – our Christian brothers and sisters – is a sign that we have passed from death to life, that is, that we have, through faith in Jesus, become part of His family (1 John 3:14,23-24).

How we show that love depends on what their needs are. It may be that they need practical help but, in difficult and alarming times, we can also show our love by encouraging each another, strengthening each other's faith, reminding each other of the promises of Scripture, of uplifting hymns and songs and other writings of God's people, of what the Lord has done in history and in our own lives. This is true comfort (see chapter 6). We can weep with those who weep (Romans 12:15 NKJV). We can help each other to be steadfast in trusting God, so as to receive more of His promised peace (Isaiah 26:3). We can even help each other to find joy in suffering (see chapter 7).

Perhaps we feel inadequate for such a great task. Yes, we are inadequate. But God helps us in our weakness and delights in using unexpected people. The more we realise our weakness, the more He can use us (2 Corinthians 12:9-10). We must be patient with ourselves and our imperfect love for others, just as we are patient with ourselves about our imperfect peace, even as we press on to become more and more Christ-like. We must not let the evil one discourage us from continuing our efforts to feel love and to show love to our brothers and sisters. Love "always protects, always trusts, always hopes, always perseveres" (1 Corinthians 13:7).

The rest of this book is divided into six chapters, each focusing on a different theme, all with the aim of lifting up the downcast. Of course, these themes overlap and run into each other, just as we have seen how love, peace and hope are connected. And who can draw a sharp line between anxiety and fear? A chapter on anxiety must touch also on the subject of peace, which we have looked at in this introduction. Many of our great hymns show how these themes gloriously blend together in the daily life of a believer (see for example pages 4-5 and 10-11). Other people, images and thoughts also recur. Three chapters mention the Bible character Job, who shows us how to emerge from terrible suffering with faith and godliness unscathed. The idea of holy mysteries that we will never fully understand on earth often applies to the Bible's message. All combine in a great kaleidoscope of separate but linked promises and encouragements to teach us that we shall not be overcome.

We shall not be overcome

In chapter 5 we will read of Bunyan's character, Mr Valiant-for-Truth, who carried with him to heaven the scars of the spiritual battles he had fought on earth, glorious trophies of his faithful witness. All of us who live for Christ will be wounded to some extent. Maybe no one but the Lord knows of secret sacrifices made for His sake, of lonely anguished decisions, of insults or betrayals – perhaps even from fellow Christians – borne in silence. Wounds may throb with pain for many years; tender scars may start to hurt whenever certain memories are evoked. Such wounds are not signs of failure but signs of faithfulness. As Amy Carmichael (1867-1951), County Down (now in Northern Ireland), who spent many years in India as a missionary, wrote

> Hast thou no scar?
> No hidden scar on foot, or side, or hand?
> I hear thee sung as mighty in the land,
> I hear them hail thy bright ascendant star,
> Hast thou no scar?
>
> Hast thou no wound?
> Yet I was wounded by the archers; spent,
> Leaned Me against a tree to die; and rent
> By ravening beasts that compassed Me, I swooned:
> Hast *thou* no wound?
>
> No wound? no scar?
> Yet, as the Master shall the servant be,
> And piercèd are the feet that follow Me;
> But thine are whole: can he have followed far
> Who has nor wound or scar?[10]

Another Christian woman, serving the Lord in a very different way, time and place, came to a similar understanding that a life lived for God is sure to be beset with difficulties, but they need not defeat us:

He did not say, "You shall not be tempest-tossed, you shall not be work-weary, you shall not be discomforted." But he said, "You shall not be overcome."[11]

2
Do not fear,
for I am with you

So do not fear, for I am with you;
  do not be dismayed, for I am your God.
I will strengthen you and help you;
  I will uphold you with my righteous right hand.

(Isaiah 41:10)

One night, as the disciples were rowing across the Sea of Galilee, a sudden storm blew up, most likely caused by an underwater earthquake, which unleashed the powerful wind, which generated the churning waves.

The disciples were frightened. They were heading, at Jesus' command to the other side of the lake, an unknown area. It was night, the time, when according to Jewish cultural belief, demons are especially active. They were on a body of water known as a Sea, and "sea" was, to the Jewish mind, a symbol of chaos and evil. And now they were lashed by a terrible tempest.

They were vulnerable - powerless in the face of impending death. Jesus, sleeping on a cushion at the back, did not stir, even when the waves breaking over the small boat began filling it with water. He seemed not to care. (Mark 4:35-41)

Many things can contribute to our fears: a sudden and overwhelming event, uncertainty about the future, a sense of powerlessness and inability to control what will happen. Sometimes fear is a useful safeguard, teaching us prudence, keeping us from sticking our hands into fires or boiling water. Perhaps this constructive "fear" should really be called "caution". But destructive fears can include a pervasive sense of dread and foreboding, a sickening sense of horror, or a sense of utter panic.

When fears arise

When fears arise
And storm clouds fill the skies,
When darkness deepens,
And sight grows dim,
And turns to endless night,
Be Thou my guide.

Lighten the darkness,
Dispel the gloom,
And in Thy presence let me hid.
Turn Thou my night to day,
Chase my fears far away
And let me there abide.

Patrick Sookhdeo, 2020[12]

The Bible has much to say about fear, and uses many different words for it. But the main message is urging us to trust in God and not to be afraid. It also gives examples of God sending panic on the enemies of His people (1 Samuel 7:10; 14:15; Zechariah 14:13), a panic which leads to their destruction.

And the Bible speaks often of another kind of "fear", the fear of the LORD, which is the beginning of wisdom (Psalm 111:10). This fear is the reverent awe that should rightly fill us as we contemplate the majesty of the God Almighty (Revelation 19:5). After Jesus had calmed the wind and waves, the frightened disciples became terrified with the fear of the Lord, as there dawned on them a new understanding of Jesus' divine power over nature.

Fear is the opposite of faith

Jesus asked the disciples in the boat why they were so afraid of the storm, why they had no faith. On another occasion he said to Jairus, about his daughter, "Don't be afraid; just believe." (Mark 5:36). For the opposite of faith is not doubt; it is fear.

As followers of Christ, we are not meant to live in the grip of destructive fear. For His perfect love casts out our fear (1 John 4:18). What is this faith that Jesus speaks of - the faith that would have kept them from fear? It is a fundamental trust in the Divine and in His purposes, knowing that we are in His hands and that God is in perfect control of every aspect of life, from earthquakes to minuscule organisms. This trust is founded on Jesus. "See, I lay a stone in Zion, a tested stone, a precious cornerstone for a sure foundation; the one who relies on it will never be stricken with panic." (Isaiah 28:16)

We all know the glorious ending of this story, when the disciples shook their Master awake and He rebuked the raging wind and waves, bringing immediate calm.

Anna Laetitia Waring (1820/23-1910), born in Wales, had a quiet but cheerful personality. She began writing poetry in her teens, learned Hebrew and read the psalms in Hebrew every day. The hymn below was one of 19 that she published in 1850 in a collection called Hymns and Meditations by A. L. W. She never married but devoted her life to philanthropic work in the Bristol area, especially prison-visiting and helping prisoners who had been released. She had a strong aversion to publicity, which is probably why little is known of her. It is believed that her last years were full of suffering and pain.

Safety in God

In heavenly love abiding,
No change my heart shall fear:
And safe is such confiding,
For nothing changes here:
The storm may roar around me,
My heart may low be laid;
But God is round about me,
And can I be dismayed?

Wherever He may guide me,
No want shall turn me back;
My Shepherd is beside me,
And nothing can I lack.
His wisdom ever waketh;
His sight is never dim;
He knows the way He taketh,
And I will walk with Him.

Green pastures are before me,
Which yet I have not seen;
Bright skies will soon be o'er me,
Where the dark clouds have been.
My hope I cannot measure;
My path to life is free;
My Saviour has my treasure,
And He will walk with me.

Anna Laetitia Waring, 1850

For the disciples, Jesus was asleep and therefore it seemed to them that He did not care what was happening. But, whilst Jesus was asleep at the stern of the boat, He was still the Son of God, and His Father neither slumbered nor slept (Psalm 121:4). His watchful eye was over them and His care for them had not ceased.

Commanded not to fear

Some three years later, as He prepared His disciples for the greatest period of uncertainty they would ever face, Jesus said to them, "Do not let your hearts be troubled. You believe in God; believe also in me." (John 14:1). He repeated His command: "Do not let your hearts be troubled and do not be afraid." (John 14:27). The word translated "troubled" in John 14 is *tarasso* (to stir up, to agitate). The same word is translated "terrified" on a later occasion when the same disciples saw Jesus walking on that same Sea of Galilee (Mark 6:50).

Our Lord Jesus is commanding us not to be afraid. In fact, the words "do not be afraid" occur 70 times in the Bible (NIV) in addition to similar phrases like "do not fear". In the New Testament the Greek word mainly used for "fear" is *phobos*, from which our English word "phobia" comes. The original meaning of *phobos* was taking flight, or running away, because of being frightened. So it has a nuance of dread, caused by intimidation or terror. *Phobos* is used of natural human fear, guilty fear, altruistic fear for the physical or spiritual welfare of others, and awe or reverence. Other relevant words are *deilia*, meaning timidity, fearfulness or cowardice, and *eulabeia* used to mean caution as well as reverence and godly fear.

The New Testament records 14 times when the reassuring command not to fear or be afraid was on Jesus' lips. For example, when walking on the unruly waters of the Sea of Galilee, He reassured His terrified disciples, saying, "Take courage! It is I. Don't be afraid." (Mark 6:50). It was the same "Don't be afraid" for Peter, when he was overcome by his own sinfulness after the miraculous catch of fishes (Luke 5:10). It was the same again for Peter, James and John at the Transfiguration (Matthew 17:7) and when He appeared in dazzling glory to John on the island of Patmos (Revelation 1:17).

With regard to persecutors, Jesus said,

> … do not be afraid of them … Do not be afraid of those who kill the body but cannot kill the soul … even the very hairs of your head are all numbered. So don't be afraid; you are worth more than many sparrows.
> (Matthew 10:26,28,30-31)

To the church of Smyrna, on the point of being severely tested by persecution, He said,

> "Do not be afraid of what you are about to suffer."
> (Revelation 2:10).

Peter, in his letter to persecuted Christians, wrote,

> Do not give way to fear … Do not fear their threats; do not be frightened.
> (1 Peter 3:6,14)

How to banish fear

But how do we obey commands like these, whether it is persecution we face or other daunting situations? How do we learn to rest in His perfect love so that our hearts are fearless and untroubled?

Face thou thy fear

Face thou thy fear
For the Saviour, He is near.

Make firm your stand
And He will grasp your hand.

Cast doubt aside
And let Him decide.

Lean on His heavenly breast,
His purposes are best.

Question not His gentle care
But see His loving tear.

Yes, see His tear-filled searching eye
For it's on you His gaze doth lie.

Patrick Sookhdeo, 2020[13]

To obey this command we must fill our hearts with Jesus. We must focus our minds on Him. Then, as the old hymn says, "the things of earth will grow strangely dim in the light of His glory and grace".[14]

We do not fear

We do not fear
Because the Saviour is near,

He who such pain did bear
For those He counts most dear.

On the cross He lay
For all my debts to pay.

Such suffering He endured
When my sins He bore.

Now in His footsteps I tread
And no curse will I dread.

Like Him I am broken bread
And with Him my blood is shed.

Patrick Sookhdeo, 2020[15]

We must ponder and meditate on the promises in God's Word and on His works in the past. We must commit them to memory, ready to draw on when we need them. The writer to the Hebrews reminded his readers of these Scriptures (Hebrews 13:5-6):

> Be strong and courageous. Do not be afraid or terrified because of them, for the LORD your God goes with you; he will never leave you nor forsake you.
>
> (Deuteronomy 31:6)

> The LORD is with me; I will not be afraid. What can mere mortals do to me? The LORD is with me; he is my helper.
>
> (Psalm 118:6-7)

The writings of Christians in times past, when wars and conflict were at least as frequent as now, when there were few cures for illnesses, when accidents were often fatal, so that sudden or early death was commonplace, can help us now. We can look out for them and note them down, creating a resource of faith-building encouragements. "Fear him, ye saints, and ye will then have nothing else to fear" wrote Brady and Tate, in their famous hymn of 1698, *Through all the changing scenes of life*.

In an age where the secular seems to control all, where humanism dominates and the fear of God is not acknowledged, we can, by God's grace, train ourselves to trust Him, to rely on His love and His power. Then we can banish negative fears and say with full assurance, whatever happens, "The LORD is with me; I will not be afraid."

Here are some ideas to help us train ourselves to trust and not to fear.

1. Discipline our minds not to give way to emotions of fear. Fill our minds with the Word of God and His promises and apply them to our own situation. "For God has not given us a spirit of fear, but of power and of love and of a sound mind." (2 Timothy 1:7 NKJV)

2. Deliberately put our trust in God. Tell Him in prayer. Speak it aloud. Sing it. "Those who know your name trust in you, for you, LORD, have never forsaken those who seek you." (Psalm 9:10)

3. Acknowledge that God is in control of our lives and nothing happens by accident. "Are not two sparrows sold for a penny? Yet not one of them will fall to the ground outside your Father's care." (Matthew 10:29)

4. Remember that God loves and cares for us. "Underneath are the everlasting arms." (Deuteronomy 33:27)

5. Embrace the Divine will, whatever comes. "Give thanks in all circumstances; for this is God's will for you in Christ Jesus." (1 Thessalonians 5:18)

6. Know the End – an eternal glory, which far outweighs "our light and momentary troubles" (2 Corinthians 4:17)

7. Care for others. "As we have opportunity, let us do good to all people, especially to those who belong to the family of believers." (Galatians 6:10)

All that is known about the author of this well-loved hymn is that his or her name began with K and that he or she appears to have been a very modest and self-effacing individual. The hymn was first published in 1787 in John Rippon's *A Selection of Hymns*, attributed simply to "K—". It reminds us of God's promises in His Word, which build our faith and take away our fear, especially Isaiah 41:10 and 43:2. The little-known penultimate verse beautifully affirms that, even when we are old and grey, our Shepherd will still gather us like lambs in his arms and carry us close to his heart (Isaiah 40:11). The emphatic last verse, and especially its resounding final line, sums everything up.

How firm a foundation

How firm a foundation, ye saints of the Lord,
Is laid for your faith in His excellent Word!
What more can He say than to you He has said,
All who unto Jesus for refuge have fled?

"In every condition – in sickness, in health,
In poverty's vale, or abounding in wealth;
At home and abroad, on the land, on the sea,
As thy days may demand shall thy strength ever be.

"Fear not, I am with thee, O be not dismayed;
I, I am thy God, and will still give thee aid:
I'll strengthen thee, help thee, and cause thee to
    stand,
Upheld by My righteous, omnipotent hand.

"When through the deep waters I call thee to go,
The rivers of grief shall not thee overflow:
For I will be with thee in trouble to bless;
And sanctify to thee they deepest distress.

"When through fiery trials they pathway shall lie,
My grace all-sufficient shall be thy supply;
The flame shall not hurt thee; I only design
Thy dross to consume, and thy gold to refine.

"E'en down to old age all my people shall prove
My sovereign, eternal, unchangeable love;
And then, when grey hairs shall their temples adorn,
Like lambs, they shall still in my bosom be borne.

"The soul that on Jesus has leaned for repose,
I will not, I will not, desert to its foes;
That soul, though all hell should endeavour to shake,
I'll never, no never, no never forsake."

Christ dispels our fear

Both the incarnation and the resurrection are studded with "fear nots". Angels encouraged Zechariah, Mary, Joseph and the shepherds with this message at the birth of our Saviour (Luke 1:13,30; Matthew 1:20; Luke 2:10) and 33 years later gave the same assurance to the bewildered women at the empty tomb (Matthew 28:5). While the guards were so afraid that they shook and fell to the ground, the women hurried away "afraid yet filled with joy" only to fall at the feet of Jesus Himself in worship. "Do not be afraid," He said to them (Matthew 28:3-10). From the beginning to the end, Christ dispels our fear.

> Why should I fear the darkest hour
> Or tremble at the tempter's power?
> Jesus vouchsafes to be my tower.
>
> I know not what may soon betide,
> Or how my wants may be supplied;
> But Jesus knows and will provide.
>
> Though sin would fill me with distress,
> The throne of grace I dare address,
> For Jesus is my righteousness.
>
> Against me earth and hell combine;
> But on my side is power divine;
> Jesus is all, and He is mine![16]

In the darkness of the night and at the centre of the roaring winds, and crashing waves, Jesus, the Son of God, was present. For God is always in the darkness. He is never absent and He does not cease to care and to intervene as He wills.

What the Bible says

Even though I walk through the darkest valley, I will
fear no evil, for you are with me; your rod and your
staff, they comfort me. (Psalm 23:4)

The Lord is my light and my salvation – whom shall I
fear? The Lord is the stronghold of my life – of whom
shall I be afraid? (Psalm 27:1)

"For I am the Lord your God who takes hold of
your right hand and says to you, Do not fear; I will
help you. Do not be afraid, you worm Jacob, little
Israel, do not fear, for I myself will help you," declares
the Lord, your Redeemer, the Holy One of Israel.
(Isaiah 41:13-14)

Do not fear, for I have redeemed you; I have
summoned you by name; you are mine. When you
pass through the waters, I will be with you; and when
you pass through the rivers they will not sweep over
you. When you walk through the fire, you will not be
burned; the flames will not set you ablaze.
(Isaiah 43:1-2)

Do not be afraid, little flock, for your Father has been
pleased to give you the kingdom. (Luke 12:32)

Do not be afraid. I am the First and the Last. I am
the Living One; I was dead, and now look, I am alive
for ever and ever! And I hold the keys of death and
Hades. (Revelation 1:17-18)

3
Coping with anxiety

Blessed is the man who trusts in the Lord,
    whose trust is the Lord.
He is like a tree planted by water,
    that sends out its roots by the stream,
and does not fear when heat comes,
    for its leaves remain green,
and is not anxious in the year of drought,
    for it does not cease to bear fruit.

(Jeremiah 17:7-8 ESV)

Early in His ministry, the Lord Jesus gathered His disciples around him on a mountainside and taught them (Matthew 5-7). The content of the "Sermon on the Mount" was astonishing and revolutionary. In one famous passage, Jesus commands "Do not worry about your life" in particular your food, clothes and health (Matthew 6:25-34). Many other translations say "Do not be anxious". This was going to be particularly relevant to the disciples who had left jobs and homes to follow Him, but is a message for us all.

The Greek word used is *merimnao*, meaning to worry anxiously - the frame of mind which gives us careworn days and sleepless nights. Jesus is not forbidding prudent forward thinking and planning, but he wants us to remain tranquil and trusting. He is telling us not to let ourselves engage in the pointless fretting that cannot change anything and may even make us literally ill with worry. This kind of worry can hinder our judgment and decision-making, or bring us to a point of paralysis where we do not dare to do anything.

Anxiety may go beyond a generalised uneasiness and become severe. Such anxiety disorders are common, well recognised mental health problems which can be very disabling. Anxiety and depression may feed off one another. Persistent worry can steal and destroy Christian joy.

Past, present and future

We often fret about the past, but the past cannot be changed. When we think of the past, it should be to look at what the Lord has done, and seek to regain our equilibrium by remembering how He has rescued us or others. The downcast psalmist ordered himself to remember God (Psalm 42:6) and that brought him comfort and reassurance. John Newton wrote in his hymn *Amazing Grace*:

> 'Tis grace hath brought me safe thus far,
> And grace will lead me home.[17]

If we feed our hearts and memories with what God has done in the past, we will not worry about the future. We can

What the Bible says

- **Command** Do not be anxious about tomorrow, for tomorrow will be anxious for itself. (Matthew 6:34 ESV)
- **Commit** Do not be anxious about anything, but in every situation, by prayer and petition, with thanksgiving, present your requests to God. (Philippians 4:6 NIV)
- **Calm** I want you to be free from anxieties. (1 Corinthians 7:32 ESV)
- **Confidence** Cast all your anxiety on him because he cares for you. (1 Peter 5:7 NIV)
- **Consider** Which of you by being anxious can add a single hour to his span of life? (Matthew 6:27 ESV)
- **Comfort** Say to those who have an anxious heart, "Be strong; fear not!" (Isaiah 35:4 ESV)
- **Cheer** Anxiety weighs down the heart, but a kind word cheers it up. (Proverbs 12:25 NIV)

also use the past as a lesson-book, to spur us and guide us in the present, so we do not replicate earlier mistakes.

Very often the present cannot be changed either. Paul advised Christian slaves not to let their lowly status worry them "although if you can gain your freedom, do so" (1 Corinthians 7:21).

The future may be full of potential difficulties, and it is easy to become anxious as we contemplate all kinds of terrible things that might or might not occur. We must remember that the Lord knows the end from the beginning, that His purposes will stand, and that He brings about what He has planned (Isaiah 46:10-11). Our lives are in His hands (John 10:28-29).

Both words and music of this hymn were the work of Edward Joy (1871-1949). He probably had in mind the words of Jesus: "Come to me, all you who are weary and burdened, and I will give you rest" (Matthew 11:28) and Peter's encouragement: "Cast all your anxiety on him because he cares for you" (1 Peter 5:7).

All Your Anxiety

Is there a heart o'erbound by sorrow?
Is there a life weighed down by care?
Come to the cross, each burden bearing;
All your anxiety—leave it there.

> *Refrain:*
> All your anxiety, all your care,
> Bring to the mercy seat, leave it there,
> Never a burden He cannot bear,
> Never a friend like Jesus!

No other friend so swift to help you,
No other friend so quick to hear,
No other place to leave your burden,
No other one to hear your prayer.

Come then at once; delay no longer!
Heed His entreaty kind and sweet,
You need not fear a disappointment;
You shall find peace at the mercy seat.

Edward H. Joy, 1920

For Christians living in contexts of persecution, as did the early Church, Jesus had a specific word of reassurance about the future:

> Whenever you are arrested and brought to trial, do not worry beforehand about what to say. Just say whatever is given you at the time, for it is not you speaking, but the Holy Spirit.

(Mark 13:11)

Care

There is another Greek word *melo*, which means almost exactly the same as *merimnao*. Together the two words, in their varying forms, are used 46 times in the New Testament. Both words could be translated "care" in the older English versions of the Bible, when "care" had the double meaning in English: (1) anxiety and worry (2) loving concern and attention. We see the first meaning in the parable of the sower, in which Jesus said that the seed that fell among the thorns was choked by the "cares of this world" (Mark 4:19 NKJV, translated as "the worries of this life" in the NIV). We see the second meaning in "He cares for you" (1 Peter 5:7) meaning that God is lovingly concerned for us. In the older translations, this short verse uses "care" in both senses: "… casting all your care [anxiety] upon Him, for He cares [has a loving concern] for you" (NKJV). Modern versions, however, tell us to cast our "anxiety" or our "worry" on Him because He cares for us. Interestingly, both *merimnao* and *melo* have the same double sense as the English "care", and so do the equivalent words in many other languages, for example, *kavalai* in

Joseph Scriven (1819-1886), an Irish immigrant to Canada, wrote this hymn in 1855 to comfort his mother in a time of special sorrow. But he himself had experienced great grief also. First, his own poor health meant that he had to give up his hope of an army career. Soon afterwards, in 1844, his fiancée died in a drowning accident on the eve of their wedding. Later that year he moved to Ontario. In 1855 he was again engaged to be married, but his fiancée fell ill and quickly died. It is little wonder that he struggled with depression and desperately needed the solace of the Lord. Scriven tried to live as literally as possible according to the teachings of the Lord Jesus in the Sermon on the Mount (Matthew 5-7). He shared all he had with others and, despite his university education, often gave his time to doing menial tasks for the poor and disabled.

What a Friend We Have in Jesus

What a friend we have in Jesus,
All our sins and griefs to bear!
What a privilege to carry
Everything to God in prayer!
Oh, what peace we often forfeit,
Oh, what needless pain we bear,
All because we do not carry
Everything to God in prayer!

Have we trials and temptations?
Is there trouble anywhere?
We should never be discouraged—
Take it to the Lord in prayer.
Can we find a friend so faithful,
Who will all our sorrows share?
Jesus knows our every weakness;
Take it to the Lord in prayer.

Are we weak and heavy-laden,
Cumbered with a load of care?
Precious Saviour, still our refuge—
Take it to the Lord in prayer.
Do thy friends despise, forsake thee?
Take it to the Lord in prayer!
In His arms He'll take and shield thee,
Thou wilt find a solace there.

Blessed Saviour, Thou hast promised
Thou wilt all our burdens bear;
May we ever, Lord, be bringing
All to Thee in earnest prayer.
Soon in glory bright, unclouded,
There will be no need for prayer—
Rapture, praise, and endless worship
Will be our sweet portion there.

Joseph Scriven, 1855

Tamil. Both meanings have in common the idea of fixed concentration on something. Concentrating on oneself leads to self-centred worry. Concentrating on others and their needs leads to forgetting of self.

Some kinds of worry can separate us from God. We have already noted the warning in the parable of the sower about the "worries of this life" which choke the growth of God's Word in us and make our lives fruitless for His Kingdom. These worries were evidently linked to riches and pleasures (Luke 8:14). Worry of this kind can become a sin. (This does not apply to anxiety as a mental illness.) We should notice that Jesus listed "the anxieties of life" along with carousing and drunkenness in a warning against things which could weigh our hearts down and leave us unprepared for His Second Coming (Luke 21:34).

We must also remember that Jesus rebuked Martha for being "worried and upset about many things" as she organised food for the guests. Surely we can imagine that Jesus spoke to her very gently and lovingly about the issue, but the fact remained that her concern for the catering meant that she had missed out on the Lord's teaching (Luke 10:38-42). It is a dilemma that often faces conscientious believers as we seek to obey the command to love others and to do everything as unto the Lord, but without becoming anxious. Paul recognises that trying to balance family responsibilities with serving the Lord can become a worry in itself and writes, "I want you to be free from anxieties." (1 Corinthians 7:32-35 ESV)

Great Christian maturity is needed to follow the simple-sounding command: "Do not be anxious about anything" (Philippians 4:6).

Seven points to help us quell our anxiety

Jesus sets out seven points to help us quell our anxiety.

1. God gave us life itself. Therefore we can trust Him for the lesser things that support our lives. If He can give us the miraculously complex human body, He can also provide food and clothes for it. (Matthew 6:25)

2. God cares for the birds, so He will surely care for us who are made in His image. This is not an invitation to laziness, for anyone who has observed birds busily building nests, one twig or wisp of straw at a time, or searching for food for themselves and their young, will know how industrious they are, albeit they do not sow, reap or store food in barns. (Matthew 6:26)

3. Worrying is pointless, fruitless and useless. It does not change the situation. (Matthew 6:27)

4. The amazing beauty that God gives to flowers, for their short lives, far beyond anything that humans can create, shows His lavish generosity and abundance. He will not run out of resources to help humankind, whom He has made "a little lower than the angels" (Psalm 8) and put to rule over the rest of His earthly creatures (Genesis 1:26). (Matthew 6:28-30)

5. Worry is natural, even logical, for those who do not know they have a loving, all-powerful heavenly Father. It should not be natural for Christians. (Matthew 6:31-32)

6. Focus on the Kingdom of God. Let that dominate our thoughts. If we fill our minds with God's purposes and glory, concentrating on how to know and do His will,

there is little thinking-time left for anxious pondering (Matthew 6:33). Jesus told us not to store up treasures on earth but to store up treasures in heaven. If our treasure is in heaven, that is where our hearts will be too (Matthew 6:19-21). A church deacon called Laurentius (Lawrence) lived in Rome in the middle of the third century, when anti-Christian persecution was severe. As a deacon, it was one of his tasks to give alms and food from the church to the poor. The Roman authorities demanded from Laurentius all the church's treasure, but Laurentius asked for three days to collect it together. During those three days he distributed everything the church possessed to the poor. Then he gathered the poor, elderly, leprosy patients and other sick and disabled and presented them to the emperor, saying that they were the treasure of the church. The furious emperor had Laurentius arrested and roasted to death.

7. Live one day at a time. Sometimes we might need to make this "Live one hour at a time." But, either way, trust God and His perfect will. Leave the future to worry about itself. (Matthew 6:34)

The serenity of Christ's followers

The fourteenth century German mystic, Johannes Tauler, met a beggar who showed the attitude that Jesus wanted His disciples to have. Tauler greeted him in the conventional way of the day: "God give you a good day, my friend."

The beggar answered, "I thank God I never had a bad one."

Then Tauler said, "God give you a happy life, my friend."

"I thank God I am never unhappy," replied the beggar. It was an amazing answer to receive from a poor and ragged beggar, so Tauler asked what he meant.

Fret not

Fret not nor care
For the Lord He is near.
He, sovereign, reigns over all,
His hand strong to deliver,
And His arm to protect
Through His mighty power.

Great is His saving mighty power,
Eternal is His everlasting love.
Infinite grace abounds,
Matchless are His works.
Sufficient for every need
Is the Lord my shield and fortress.

My shield and my strong fortress He shall be,
When through the darkness I cannot see
And though fiery darts and snares abound
His promise He will keep
My every need to meet,
He'll never leave me nor forsake.

He never leaves, He's always near.
His presence will sustain,
In every circumstance and trial.
Though mountains quake and winds roar
I cast my cares upon Him
And fret not.

Patrick Sookhdeo, 2020[18]

"Well," said the beggar, "When it is fine, I thank God; when it rains, I thank God; when I have plenty, I thank God; when I am hungry, I thank God; and, since God's will is my will, and whatever pleases him pleases me, why should I say I am unhappy when I am not?"

Astonished, Tauler asked the beggar, "What are you?"

"I am a king," said the beggar.

"Where, then, is your kingdom?" asked Tauler.

The beggar replied quietly "In my heart."

The bottom line is that Christ's followers should be people marked by serenity and contentment, whatever their circumstances. For worry is a characteristic of pagans (Matthew 6:32). But we are blessed with the knowledge that we have a loving heavenly Father who knows our needs before we ask Him (Matthew 6:8). With Isaiah, we can declare to our Father: "You will keep in perfect peace those whose minds are steadfast, because they trust in You." (Isaiah 26:3). If we can lay aside anxiety, we will find not only greater peace of heart but also greater power to live effectively for the Lord and to build His Kingdom.

Paul gives us a promise that can build our faith and end our anxiety if we truly take it to heart.

> My God will meet all your needs according to the riches of his glory in Christ Jesus (Philippians 4:19)

One who must have fully absorbed this promise was George Müller (1805-98), who never requested funding for the orphanages he established in Bristol, UK; he only prayed that God would provide. Sometimes it looked as if the orphans were going to have to go hungry, but always a gift of food or money was received just in time. Müller said: "The beginning of anxiety is the end of faith, and the beginning of true faith is the end of anxiety."

Leaning on the everlasting arms, by the prolific hymn writer Elisha Albright Hoffman (1839-1929), is an encouraging and timeless hymn of trust and endurance in the face of troubles encountered in the Christian's everyday earthly pilgrimage.

Leaning on the everlasting arms

What a fellowship, what a joy divine,
leaning on the everlasting arms;
what a blessedness, what a peace is mine,
leaning on the everlasting arms.

> *Refrain:*
> Leaning, leaning,
> safe and secure from all alarms;
> leaning, leaning,
> leaning on the everlasting arms.

O how sweet to walk in this pilgrim way,
leaning on the everlasting arms;
O how bright the path grows from day to day,
leaning on the everlasting arms.

What have I to dread, what have I to fear,
leaning on the everlasting arms?
I have blessed peace with my Lord so near,
leaning on the everlasting arms.

Verses by E. A. Hoffman (1887), added to refrain
written earlier by Anthony J Showalter

4
Trusting God in Uncertain Times

Surely God is my salvation;
    I will trust and not be afraid.
The Lord, the Lord himself, is my strength
and my defence;
    he has become my salvation.'

(Isaiah 12:2)

The world we live in seems to grow ever more tumultuous, the future ever more uncertain. Disease and death, war and conflict, mighty nations flexing their muscles, violence and exploitation, economic and natural disasters, intolerance and persecution … Only God knows what will happen next.

But, no matter our circumstances, we ought to guard our relationship with the Lord and build ourselves up in our faith (Jude v20). For there is spiritual peril both in times of ease and plenty and in times of hardship and danger. Agur prayed:

... give me neither poverty nor riches,
  but give me only my daily bread.
Otherwise, I may have too much and disown you
and say, "Who is the Lord?"
Or I may become poor and steal,
  and so dishonour the name of my God.

(Proverbs 30:8-9)

On one side lie the dangers for some of despair, anger towards God, loss of faith and the temptation to use sinful methods for personal survival. On the other side lie the dangers for some of arrogance, spiritual complacency and the temptation to put our trust in material things and human power instead of in our God. How then should we live?[19]

Whatever happens, we should make God a priority, trusting Him every day and all day long. Many of us spend a little time with God in the early morning, but then we put Him aside to continue our day. Here are four ways that we can learn to trust Him moment by moment.

Live a life of desire towards God

Let our souls thirst for Him "as the deer pants for streams of water" (Psalm 42:1). We long to behold His beauty and taste His goodness. There is nothing we desire in heaven or earth more than Him, and we yearn to know Him better, love Him better, and be more conformed to His will and likeness.

We would do well to pray for this first thing in the morning, asking that the burning desire for Him remain with us throughout the day, guiding our every thought, word and action. In this way, our desire will be like the fire that was always kept burning on the Old Testament altar (Leviticus 6:12), ready at any time for sacrifices to be offered on it. This is one of the main ways in which we can fulfil the Biblical command to pray without ceasing (1 Thessalonians 5:17).

Live a life of delight in God

While we desire more and more of God and long to see Him face to face, at the same time we can already delight in Him and be satisfied with Him, finding rest in Him as our thoughts dwell on Him. We can delight in His character, His creation, His covenant, His promises, His salvation.

We should have greater pleasure in thinking about our God than a lover has in thinking about their human beloved, or a miser has in thinking about their store of money. Turning our thoughts to God should be an antidote to any sorrow, worry or disappointment.

Live a life of dependence on God

Trusting God means that we look to Him for provision of all good that comes to us and for protection from all evil that threatens us. Guided and grounded in the promises given to us within His Word, we can be humbly confident, with full assurance of faith.

But what about the times when "the olive crop fails and the fields produce no food ... there are no sheep in the sheepfold and no cattle in the stalls" (Habakkuk 3:17) or when Covid-19 lockdown reduces our income to zero? This is when a "holy habit" of trusting God yields its most precious fruit. For it enables us to keep trusting, even in the most desperate situations, and to affirm with Job, "Though he slay me, yet will I trust in him" (Job 13:15 KJV).

Live a life of devotedness to God

This is the life of the devoted servant, ready at every moment to do the master's will, or to work to advance his cause and his honour. It is "waiting on God" in the way that, many centuries ago, a lady-in-waiting would wait on the Queen she served, remaining always close at hand to her mistress, poised and ready to act. This kind of devotedness lays aside our own will and says always "Thy will be done." We make His will our rule.

The Welsh Presbyterian minister Matthew Henry (1662-1714) wrote:

> It is the character of the redeemed of the Lord,
> that they follow the Lamb wheresoever he goes,
> with an implicit faith and obedience. As the eyes
> of a servant are to the hand of his master, and
> the eyes of a maiden to the hand of her mistress,
> so must our eyes wait on the Lord, to do what
> he appoints us, to take what he allots us ...[20]

Accepting God's providence

We have already seen that trusting the Lord involves making the will of His precept the rule of our practice. But we should also "make the will of his providence the rule of our patience"[21] and bear whatever afflictions come our way with a trustful spirit. The deep and mysterious truth that "all things work together for good to them that love God, to them who are the called according to his purpose" (Romans 8:28 KJV) is something that we ought to embrace with our whole being, rather than simply acknowledge with our minds.

Let us learn from Christian brothers and sisters who live with poverty and persecution how to respond to tribulations in a properly Christian way, that is, a way in which our trust in our heavenly Father remains unshaken despite our troubles.

The German pastor Dietrich Bonhoeffer (1906-45) wrote from prison in Nazi Germany, shortly before his execution:

> And when the cup you give is filled to brimming
> With bitter suffering, hard to understand,
> We take it gladly, trusting though with trembling,
> Out of so good and so beloved a hand.[22]

Amy Carmichael wrote a poem about the various ways someone might react to try to deal with a great sorrow that had come upon them, but only one way was effective – to accept the inexplicable suffering from God:

> He said, "I will accept the breaking sorrow
> Which God to-morrow
> Will to His son explain."
> Then did the turmoil deep within him cease.
> *Not vain the word, not vain;*
> *For in Acceptance lieth peace.*[23]

When Job had lost his ten children and his vast wealth, and was covered with sores from head to foot, he refused his wife's suggestion of cursing God. Instead he declared, "Shall we accept good from God, and not trouble?" (Job 2:10)

Let us remember that God is also the sustainer of all His creation. As we look for the work of God's providence in the world around us, let us not be too preoccupied with ourselves but look outward to those around us, all of whom are created and loved by Him.

A meditation on trusting in God through times of trial and tribulation. Seeing through the "eye of faith" helps us accept the ultimate good of all God's providence, even pain and suffering. His love for us is enduring and eternal, in times of darkness and light.

Whether seen or unseen

[1]Darkness, deepening
   darkness,
Fear, deepening fear,
Taking possession of the
   soul.
Shrouding with hopelessness
Wrapping in despair.

[2]God removed, absent,
   Hidden by the clouds.
Light dispelled by blackest
   night,
Yet God remains,
Seen by the eye of faith.

[3]For God is in the darkness,
   His presence in the shadows,
Unseen, He is there,
His guiding hand
Leading in the night.

[4]So, my soul,
   Put your trust in God.
Whether seen or unseen,
His love will remain
And be ever the same.

[5]His purposes are good
And in time the clouds will lift,
The darkness be dispelled,
And He in glorious light
Will turn night into day.

Patrick Sookhdeo, 2020[24]

Living in God's presence

If we long to trust God fully, all day, every day, desiring Him, delighting in Him, depending on Him and devoted to Him, how can we learn to do this? We know that His eye is always upon us, wherever we are and whatever we are doing, but how can we learn to accept both our comforts and our crosses from His hand, with an unwavering trust? Perhaps the following thoughts and reflections can help us.

Continually trusting and waiting on God

Although ladies-in-waiting have days off from their work, we – like the angels in heaven – wait on God continually. We are bond-servants who neither want nor expect to be discharged from our duties. Indeed, this is our joyful and glorious destiny in eternity – to serve the Lamb (Revelation 22:3).

We should trust God *seven days a week*. On Sundays it is easier to spend time with God, as we worship Him with others, and especially if we are able to rest from our daily work. But the spiritual resources with which we strengthen ourselves on a Sunday can be drawn on to help us throughout the next six days to continue trusting God. In the words of Matthew Henry, we "must be so in the Spirit on the Lord's Day, as to walk in the Spirit all the week."[25]

Keeping God our focus in all circumstances and seasons

Whether busy or relaxing, we do well to remember the Lord. Even on days of frantic busy-ness, when our hands and minds may be fully occupied, our hearts can still be focused on Him, through a habitual concern for His glory and a habitual recognition of His providential hand at work (Romans 12:2). When we are relaxing we also need to take care that we do not forget the Lord (Psalm 63:6). So-called "me-time" should be "Him-time" just as much as any other time is.

In prosperity and in adversity alike, we trust God (Job 1:21; Philippians 4:12). When the world smiles on us, it is the One who has provided for us who deserves our thanks. We should continually ask His blessing and favour, as well as His guidance, wisdom and grace to use for His glory and purposes what He has entrusted to us. When the world frowns on us, let us not give way to fret or fear but continue to trust. We can bring our afflictions to the throne of God, asking that He will use the experience to help us mature in faith and grow in Christlikeness.

Perhaps some of us have considerable experience of joyfully receiving good things and less experience of patiently accepting hard things as part of God's providence – if so, we can ask for grace to learn the Christ-like patience that is part of the fruit of the Spirit. (Galatians 5:22)

We are called to trust God in youth and in old age. No one is too young to serve the Lord. The story of attentive little Samuel, who heard the Lord's call, is well known (1 Samuel 3). But elsewhere, too, the Bible commends those who are mindful of their Creator and remember Him despite the distractions of youth (Ecclesiastes 12:1). Some societies discard the elderly as useless, but in God's economy they are as valued as ever. Matthew Henry reminds us of their role as precious "waiting servants":

> When through the infirmities of age they can no longer be working servants in God's family, they may be waiting servants ... Those who have done the will of God, and their doing work is at an end, have need of patience to

enable them to wait till they inherit the promise; and the nearer the happiness is which they are waiting for, the dearer should the God be they are waiting on, and hope shortly to be with, to be with eternally.[26]

Indeed, long years of practice should make older believers the best guides for the rest of us regarding how to wait trustingly on God. The prophetess Anna was one example (Luke 2:36-37) and we probably all know others. Let us ask them to teach us what they have learned.

Wisdom for our day-to-day cares and duties

As we have already considered in chapter 3, we are exhorted to cast our daily cares on God so that they do not distract us from trusting Him. For some of us this process of "casting our cares on Him" will have to be repeated numerous times through the day, whether it is the same worry that comes creeping back again and again to nag away at our minds, or a plethora of fresh problems descending on us. (1 Peter 5:7 KJV)

We should manage our daily business for Him. Whatever our task, whoever our earthly employer, ultimately we are working for God. Remembering this moment by moment will sanctify even the most ordinary actions, as we do everything as if for the Lord Jesus and in His Name (Colossians 3:17,23) and in His strength (Philippians 4:13).

We do well to receive our daily needs and comforts as from Him, calling to mind as often as we can that it is our heavenly Father who gives us not only our daily bread, shelter, clothes and similar basic needs but all other blessings too. Every breath we draw and every step we take is only possible because of His grace and mercy. (Psalm 103:1-5)

We strive to resist our daily temptations by His grace. As long as we live on earth, sin is crouching at the door and longs to master us (Genesis 4:7). The evil one will seek many times a day to trip us and trap us, yet we can turn every time to the Lord for His strength to resist. (1 Corinthians 10:13)

We should do our daily duties in the strength of the Lord. "Duty" is an unfashionable word in the twenty-first century and "good works" are often mocked or mistrusted. But those who live their lives looking trustfully to God are always alert to the opportunities that He gives for service, both large and small – a cheerful word here, a helping hand there. They are eager to do whatever they can for Him.

Guarding against spiritual weariness

There is a danger that we will "become weary in doing good" (Galatians 6:9), dejected, listless and discouraged. We may cease to feel much empathy for the suffering of others or to feel righteous anger about injustice. Prayer, worship and reading the Bible may begin to seem like meaningless mechanical exercises.

This sluggishness of heart was called *acedia* by the early Christians, a Greek word literally meaning "not caring". Even towering spiritual heroes can be overtaken by *acedia*, especially after a time of great stress, exertion or persecution. Elijah (1 Kings 19:4) and Jeremiah (Jeremiah 20:17-18) are two examples. John the Baptist was apparently overwhelmed by doubts while in prison (Matthew 11:3).

In these situations we ought not to yield to inner discouragement, but strive to conquer it. "We do not lose heart," said Paul with determination in the midst of afflictions (2 Corinthians 4:1,16). So, we do not give up seeking to walk closely with Him, to hear His voice and do His will, for He has promised to renew our strength (Isaiah 40:29-31).

Bearing our afflictions

We should bear our daily afflictions with submission to His will. Troubles and grief are to be expected, for Jesus said that His followers must take up their cross daily (Luke 9:23), and warned that in this world we will have trouble (John 16:33), most likely including persecution (John 15:18-20). We should accept these afflictions as the will of God, and as a means to grow in grace and holiness. Perhaps we will have to remind ourselves of this truth many times a day, particularly if we wrestle with physical pain or sickness.

As we consider daily news we do well to trust in the Lord and seek to discern His will and purposes. Through His wisdom we can see events in the world around us, and in our own personal lives, from an eternal perspective (Psalm 33:9-11). Trusting in God will mean that if our hopes are fulfilled, they will not distract us from Him. Equally, trusting Him will mean that if our hopes are deferred they will not make our hearts sick.

We need to remind ourselves continually that our God is all-powerful, all-knowing and all-loving. Although we often do not understand His ways, we can always trust Him.

5
Death
and our sure hope of heaven

Precious in the sight of the LORD
is the death of his faithful servants.

(Psalm 116:15)

For some, death is the unmentionable subject. People often view their future death with fear or resentment. As it draws nearer, they rage against it, saying they have not enjoyed their lives enough yet, have not accomplished everything on their "bucket list", or will miss their loved ones. Yet death (*thanatos* in Greek) is mentioned frequently in the New Testament – 120 times, in fact – and the verb "die" (*apothnesko* or *thnesko*) another 120 times.

death (James 1:15). Even God's law brings death, because we cannot keep the law properly (Romans 7:9-13). In Revelation we read of the "second death", meaning ultimate separation from God, after the first death, our physical death (Revelation 2:11; 20:6,14; 21:8).

The message of the New Testament is that Jesus Christ delivers us from spiritual death.

> He himself bore our sins in his body on the cross, so that we might die to sins and live for righteousness; by his wounds you have been healed.
>
> (1 Peter 2:24)

Through Jesus' own death and resurrection, the power of death has been destroyed, and those who trust in Him will be safe on the Day of Judgment and for all eternity. Many favourite hymns reflect this deliverance, for example, *Rock of Ages*, which Prince Albert, husband of Queen Victoria, asked for as he lay on his deathbed in 1861. When the *SS London*, sailing from England to Australia, sank in a storm in January 1866 only one lifeboat could be successfully launched, leaving 244 people on board. The 19 in the lifeboat heard those on the ship singing *Rock of Ages*, as the *London* upended and plunged into the waves.

> While I draw this fleeting breath,
> When my eyelids close in death,
> When I soar through tracts unknown,
> See thee on thy judgement throne,
> Rock of ages, cleft for me,
> Let me hide myself in thee.[27]

What the Bible says

I am the resurrection and the life. The one who believes in me will live, even though they die; and whoever lives by believing in me will never die.

(John 11:25-26)

For God so loved the world that he gave his one and only Son, that whoever believes in him shall not perish but have eternal life.

(John 3:16)

Very truly I tell you, whoever hears my word and believes him who sent me has eternal life and will not be judged but has crossed over from death to life.

(John 5:24)

For to me, to live is Christ and to die is gain.

(Philippians 1:21)

I know that my redeemer lives, and that in the end he will stand on the earth. And after my skin has been destroyed, yet in my flesh I will see God; I myself will see him with my own eyes—I, and not another. How my heart yearns within me!

(Job 19:25-27)

He has also set eternity in the human heart

(Ecclesiastes 3:11)

Praise be to the God and Father of our Lord Jesus Christ! In his great mercy he has given us new birth into a living hope through the resurrection of Jesus Christ from the dead, and into an inheritance that can never perish, spoil or fade. This inheritance is kept in heaven for you,

(1 Peter 1:3-4)

… I am convinced that neither death nor life, neither angels nor demons, neither the present nor the future, nor any powers, neither height nor depth, nor anything else in all creation, will be able to separate us from the love of God that is in Christ Jesus our Lord.

(Romans 8:38-39)

Then I heard a voice from heaven say, "Write this: blessed are the dead who die in the Lord from now on."

"Yes," says the Spirit, "they will rest from their labour, for their deeds will follow them."

(Revelation 14:13)

It is through the death of His Son that we can be reconciled with God (Romans 5:10; Colossians 1:22). We shall never experience Revelation's "second death" if we trust in Jesus John 8:51; 11:25-26) for we have passed from death to life (John 5:24; 1 John 3:14). If we help someone to repent and put their faith in Christ, we save them from spiritual death (James 5:20). As a famous hymn puts it, using the imagery of crossing the river Jordan to reach the promised land, Canaan:

> Death of death and hell's destruction
> Land me safe on Canaan's side[28]

All through the New Testament, we read wonderful words affirming Jesus' victory over death. "It was impossible for death to keep its hold on him," declared Peter on the Day of Pentecost. He "has destroyed death and has brought life and immortality," wrote Paul to Timothy (2 Timothy 1:10), and to the Christians in Rome he wrote that "death no longer has mastery over him" (Romans 6:9). The writer to the Hebrews said that, by his death, Christ broke the power of "him who holds the power of death – that is, the devil" and thus set free "those who all their lives were held in slavery by their fear of death". (Hebrews 2:14-15) This victory can be ours too!

> The sting of death is sin, and the power of sin is
> the law. But thanks be to God! He gives us the
> victory through our Lord Jesus Christ.
>
> (1 Corinthians 15:56-57)

In the early Church the sign of the cross was considered a "sign of victory" or *tropaion*, the term used by the Greek-speaking ancient world for a triumphal sign set up to mark the place where the turning point in a victorious battle had occurred. A *tropaion* was usually a vertical tree-trunk or post, sometimes with a pair of outstretched branches, like arms, on which the armour of the defeated enemy was hung. For Christians, the cross is a *tropaion* for the faithful, marking the place where victory over death was won.

When the night of this world is past...

Just as we remember our birthday every year, when our earthly lives began, so we should remember regularly that there will be a day when our earthly lives come to an end. As Christian believers, we could look on that day as our second birthday, or perhaps our third birthday - after the day we were born and the day we were born again. For, in the wise words of Bede in eighth-century England,

> Christ is the morning star who when the night of this world is past brings to his saints the promise of the light of life and opens everlasting day.[29]

In a long and glorious passage on the resurrection of the dead, the apostle Paul writes repeatedly of death as "falling asleep", after which we are raised imperishable and immortal. It is so exciting one can hardly wait. (1 Corinthians 15:12-57) Small wonder that Paul wrote elsewhere of his great desire to depart this life and be with Christ (Philippians 1:21-24).

C.S. Lewis called death a "farewell to shadowlands" and the beginning of "Chapter One of the Great Story which

Henri Abraham César Malan (1787-1864) was born in Switzerland, to a family of French Protestants whose earlier generations had fled anti-Protestant persecution in France. Malan became a passionate evangelist, preaching the Gospel in Switzerland, France, Belgium and Britain, and writing numerous tracts, pamphlets and hymns. This hymn, *Non, ce n'est pas mourir que d'aller vers son Dieu*, is perhaps based on the Apostle Paul's declaration that "we would rather be away from the body and at home with the Lord" 2 Corinthians 5:8), It was translated into English by the American pastor and scholar George Washington Bethune (1805-62).

It is not death to die

[1]It is not death to die,
  to leave this weary road,
  and, 'midst the brotherhood
    on high,
  to be at home with God.

[2]It is not death to close
  the eye long dimmed by
    tears,
  and wake in glorious repose,
  to spend eternal years.

[3]It is not death to bear
  the wrench that sets us free
  from dungeon-chain, to
    breathe the air
  of boundless liberty.

[4]It is not death to fling
  aside this sinful dust,
  and rise, on strong, exulting
    wing,
  to live among the just.

[5]Jesus, thou Prince of Life!
  thy chosen cannot die!
  Like thee, they conquer in the strife,
  to reign with thee on high.

César Malan, 1832, translated by George. W. Bethune, 1847

no one on earth has read: which goes on for ever: in w every chapter is better than the one before."[30]

Death is the gateway to our heavenly life in our resurrection bodies. It opens the way to blessed rest from our troubles, sorrows and afflictions and from the weary spiritual battle and storms of life in a fallen world. Charles Wesley's beautiful hymn, *Jesus, Lover of my Soul*, expresses this homecoming to peace and security:

> Hide me, O my Saviour, hide,
> Till the storm of life is past;
> Safe into the haven guide;
> O receive my soul at last.[31]

In John Bunyan's *Pilgrim's Progress*, Mr Valiant-for-Truth is covered with scars from the wounds he has received in the hard spiritual battle he has fought during this life. But then the time comes for him to die, or, in the imagery of Bunyan, to cross the river on the other side of which is heaven:

> When he understood it, he called for his friends,
> and told them of it. Then said he, I am going to
> my Father's; and though with great difficulty I
> am got hither, yet now I do not repent me of all
> the trouble I have been at to arrive where I am.
> My sword I give to him that shall succeed me in
> my pilgrimage, and my courage and skill to him
> that can get it. My marks and scars I carry with
> me, to be a witness for me that I have fought
> His battles who now will be my rewarder. When
> the day that he must go hence was come, many
> accompanied him to the river-side, into which as

he went he said, "*Death, where is thy sting?*" And,
as he went down deeper, he said, "*Grave, where
is thy victory?*" So he passed over, and all the
trumpets sounded for him on the other side.[32]

Mr Valiant-for-Truth had no doubts or fears about
what awaited him after crossing the river. He knew that
he would find himself in heaven, our promised land. The
Scriptures contain many assurances for Christian believers
that, after the death of our bodies, we will be with the
Lord for ever. This is often called our Christian hope. We
must remember that "hope" in the New Testament has a
different meaning from its everyday usage. It does not mean
a longed-for possibility that might or might not happen.
It means a confident expectation, a happy looking forward
to something that is certain to take place. So the Christian
hope is a sure hope on which we can utterly depend, based
on the reality of the resurrected Christ.

> We have this hope as an anchor for the soul, firm
> and secure.
>
> (Hebrews 6:19)

We also have the Holy Spirit as a pledge or deposit or down
payment, guaranteeing "what is to come".

> Now it is God who makes both us and you stand
> firm in Christ. He anointed us, set his seal of
> ownership on us, and put his Spirit in our hearts
> as a deposit, guaranteeing what is to come.
>
> (2 Corinthians 1:21-22)

> When you believed, you were marked in him
> with a seal, the promised Holy Spirit, who is a
> deposit guaranteeing our inheritance until the
> redemption of those who are God's possession
> (Ephesians 1:13-14)

We need have no fear of what comes after the grave. God graciously tells us in His Word something of what heaven will be like, using many different images. (See pages 74-75.) Of course, our merely human minds cannot really conceive what life in our imperishable, spiritual, resurrection bodies will be like. A caterpillar, crawling stolidly along a twig, surely cannot begin to visualise or comprehend life as a butterfly, soaring freely in the air. The difference between our earthly lives and our heavenly lives will be much greater than this. But the Bible gives us thrilling hints and glimpses and pictures, and the Holy Spirit helps us understand.

> "What no eye has seen, nor ear heard,
>   nor the heart of man imagined,
> what God has prepared for those who love him"—
> these things God has revealed to us through the
>   Spirit.
> (1 Corinthians 2:9-10 ESV)

Eternal life

We already have a foretaste of heaven, even here on earth. For in the moment when we put our trust in Christ, we receive eternal life.

What the Bible says

Then I saw a new heaven and a new earth, for the first heaven and the first earth had passed away, and there was no longer any sea. I saw the Holy City, the new Jerusalem, coming down out of heaven from God, prepared as a bride beautifully dressed for her husband. And I heard a loud voice from the throne saying, 'Look! God's dwelling-place is now among the people, and he will dwell with them. They will be his people, and God himself will be with them and be their God. He will wipe every tear from their eyes. There will be no more death or mourning or crying or pain, for the old order of things has passed away.'

(Revelation 21:1-4)

Then the angel showed me the river of the water of life, as clear as crystal, flowing from the throne of God and of the Lamb down the middle of the great street of the city. On each side of the river stood the tree of life, bearing twelve crops of fruit, yielding its fruit every month. And the leaves of the tree are for the healing of the nations. No longer will there be any curse. The throne of God and of the Lamb will be in the city, and his servants will serve him. They will see his face, and his name will be on their foreheads. There will be no more night. They will not need the light of a lamp or the light of the sun, for the Lord God will give them light. And they will reign for ever and ever.

(Revelation 22:1-5)

After this I looked, and there before me was a great multitude that no-one could count, from every nation, tribe, people and language, standing before the throne and before the Lamb. They were wearing white robes and were holding palm branches in their hands. And they cried out in a loud voice:

> 'Salvation belongs to our God,
> who sits on the throne,
> and to the Lamb.'

All the angels were standing round the throne and round the elders and the four living creatures. They fell down on their faces before the throne and worshipped God.

(Revelation 7:9-11)

You make known to me the path of life; you will fill me with joy in your presence, with eternal pleasures at your right hand.

(Psalm 16:11)

On this mountain the Lord Almighty will prepare a feast of rich food for all peoples, a banquet of aged wine – the best of meats and the finest of wines. On this mountain he will destroy the shroud that enfolds all peoples, the sheet that covers all nations; he will swallow up death for ever. The Sovereign Lord will wipe away the tears from all faces; he will remove his people's disgrace from all the earth. The Lord has spoken.

(Isaiah 25:6-8)

Very truly I tell you, the one who believes
has eternal life.

(John 6:47)

"Eternal life" is a phrase that occurs mainly in the writings of John. (Other New Testament authors often say simply "life" to mean the same thing.[33]) "Eternal life", meaning "the life of the age to come", indicates the nature of our life, not its duration. It is the life of heaven.

But Jesus taught that the nature of life in the future age (the next world) can, through Him, be experienced here and now. Eternal life is a gift from Him to us (John 17:2), if we believe in Him (John 3:15-16,36). Jesus does not say that we need vast quantities of faith, only that our faith, however small it may be, must be in Him. We do not have to wait until we have left this world to receive His gift of eternal life (John 6:54) for we possess it here and now. We have already crossed over from death to life and will not be condemned on the Day of Judgment (John 5:24).

Because of their relationship with Christ, every believer alive today already possesses eternal life. Because of the resurrection of Christ, this will one day be extended to the sphere of their body (2 Corinthians 5:4; 2 Timothy 1:10).

A beautiful old hymn tells us:

Blessed assurance, Jesus is mine;
Oh, what a foretaste of glory divine![34]

So, what are the heavenly characteristics of the eternal life that we have already, even while we still struggle with earthly life? Jesus described it like this:

> ... this is eternal life: that they know you, the only
> true God, and Jesus Christ, whom you have sent.
>
> (John 17:3)

Heaven, the dwelling-place of God where He lives among and with His people, has nothing impure within it. There will be no sea and no night – those Biblical symbols of chaos and sin. (Revelation 21:1,3,22-27) Just as death and sin are linked, life and holiness are linked.

So eternal life is a life of fellowship with God, in holiness and righteousness, whether on earth or in heaven. In the words of Richard Chenevix Trench,

> Scripture [knows] of no higher word than *zoe*
> [life] to set forth the blessedness of God and
> the blessedness of the creature in communion
> with God.[35]

We live with the reality of eternal life now and the sure and certain hope of heaven to come. When we face physical death we shall not be going to an unknown place. We shall simply be stepping from our earthly life to our heavenly life. We shall be going home, to see our beloved Lord face to face at last.

Being ready

Instead of shrinking from the thought of death, we should follow the example of Christians who lived in times far more uncertain than our present era, times when early death from illness, accident or violence was always likely. These Christians thought often of death and kept themselves in a state of readiness. Matthew Henry wrote:

> It is good for us to think familiarly of dying, to
> think of it as our going to bed, that by thinking
> often of it, and thinking thus of it, we may get
> above the fear of it.[36]

What habits of thought can we embrace so as to make ourselves comfortable with the knowledge of our mortality?

1.   Death is like retiring to the privacy of our own bedrooms to lie down for a night's sleep. Every morning we rise from our beds and go out to mix with people again. In the same way, death is a solo experience, but we shall meet our loved ones again in the morning of the resurrection. When we say goodbye to them on earth, it is only like saying "good night" in the evening, knowing that we will greet them again next day.

2.   At death we leave behind our earthly bodies, just as we take off our clothes to sleep. Some of us have bodies that are a great burden, whether through sickness, frailty, failing faculties or disability. Some of us also have mental illnesses that distress us and weigh us down. At death we leave behind all such hindrances, just like taking off cumbersome, scratchy, badly-fitting clothes. What a joy and relief! In the morning we shall find a beautiful new set of clothes in which our souls can dress for eternity. (Job 1:21; 2 Corinthians 5:2-4)

3.   At death we shall lie down in the grave as we lie on our beds, but – being forgiven sinners – we shall rest in peace (Isaiah 57:2). There will be no tossing and turning, no nightmares. The grave is a bed of spices (Song of Songs 6:2). We shall rise from it, completely refreshed, to meet our soul's Beloved and be with Him for ever.

So we could follow the example of some of the saints of old and use these three daily events – going to our bedroom, undressing, lying down – to remind ourselves of death, that it is inevitable, that it might come tonight, and that it is the gateway to heaven. Before falling asleep we could prayerfully commit ourselves into God's hands, as if it were our last prayer.

A prayer in the hour of death

In this hour of my death
I entrust myself into Your loving care.
Release me, O Lord,
From all fear and anxiety.
Give me that trust and confidence
To embrace You, my Lord.
Give me that faith to see
The heavenly kingdom that awaits me.
To You I commit now my soul.
Forgive me my many sins and failures
By Your great mercy.
Take my hand,
O my beloved Lord,
And lead me Home
So that when I awake
I awake with You.

Amen

Patrick Sookhdeo, 2020[37]

6
True comfort

For the LORD comforts his people
and will have compassion on his afflicted ones.

(Isaiah 49:13)

'I, even I, am he who comforts you.

(Isaiah 51:12)

The longing for comfort has never been more urgent. Many
in our world are living with pain and sorrow and uncertainty.
Many are mired in degrading poverty and endure a gruelling
struggle with daily hunger. Some are lonely and isolated, with
friends and family out of reach. Perhaps they face their final days
and hours with no one but strangers around their bedside. When
the Covid-19 pandemic was first spreading around the globe,
even the solace of a funeral at which to mourn loved ones and
celebrate their lives was impossible for some.

The pressure that we experience is like being in a confined space, or having a heavy weight placed upon us. We long for the relief and release of entering a spacious place, and also to know that God is present with His people, and can bring them encouragement, hope and comfort.

Paul's second letter to the Corinthians is the letter in which, more than any other, he reveals his heart, his emotions, and above all his sufferings, and it begins with a most striking description of God. Paul speaks of God as "the Father of compassion and the God of all comfort" (2 Corinthians 1:3). Ultimately, it is God's very nature to bring succour and help to His afflicted people. The short passage (v.3-7) resounds with repetition of the word "comfort" (ten times in the original Greek, nine times in most English translations) interwoven with words for suffering and affliction (seven times). Paul derives great comfort, strength and reassurance from knowing that God Himself is the source of all his comfort, albeit channelled to him through Christian brothers and sisters.

But what does "comfort" mean? Some English words have changed their meaning dramatically. Today the word "comfort" has a "soft and fluffy" feel to it, but in the fourteenth century, when John Wycliffe was translating the Bible, it was a robust and powerful term. Most of its broad range of meanings have now disappeared, leaving little but the idea of soothing and consoling with sympathetic words. It has become a mundane, everyday word, with little substance.

In order to understand the word "comfort" in the Bible, we need to banish from our minds modern ideas such as quilts, warm scarves or baby's dummies. We should not think of reassuring blankets, cosy armchairs or easy lifestyles.

The "fort" part of the word "comfort" comes from the Latin *fortis*, which has two meanings (1) physical strength (2) courage and steadfastness. "Fortitude" is another English word that comes from *fortis*. So the old meaning of "comforting" someone was to make them strong and brave to endure. Wycliffe even translated Ephesians 6:10 as "Be ye comforted in the Lord", which to him meant "Be empowered in the Lord." It was William Tyndale in the fifteenth century who first gave us "Be strong in the Lord."

To help us better understand God's Word to us, we can look carefully at the meanings of the Hebrew and Greek vocabulary used in the original Bible texts and later translated as "comfort".

Comfort, comfort my people

The most famous use of the word "comfort" in the Old Testament is surely the command:

> Comfort, comfort my people, says your God.
> Speak tenderly to Jerusalem, and proclaim to her
> that her hard service has been completed, that
> her sin has been paid for, that she has received
> from the Lord's hand double for all her sins.
>
> (Isaiah 40:1-2).

Based on this text, "comfort" resounds thrillingly as the first word of Handel's magnificent oratorio *Messiah*.

The Hebrew word is *nachamu* from which the names Nehemiah and Nahum come. Its literal meaning is "to cause to breathe again", letting one's breath out in relief. It is a word of great emotion, and certainly includes the idea of consolation in grief, as we can see in other parts of the Old Testament (e.g. Genesis 37:35; 1 Chronicles 7:22; Jeremiah 31:15). But it means more. It also describes a process of learning to think differently about a situation. A rabbi explains: "Comfort begins when we can reframe the immediate pain of a loss in a larger,

Little is known of Katharina von Schlegel, author of this evangelical Lutheran hymn of comfort and consolation. It was a great favourite of the Scottish athlete Eric Liddell (1902-45), who came to the world's attention at the 1924 Olympics for refusing to run on a Sunday. Liddell later became a missionary in China, where he was taken prisoner by the Japanese military during World War II. He is thought to have taught this hymn to others in the internment camp for enemy nationals, before he died there of a brain tumour on 21 February 1945.

Be Still, My Soul

Be still, my soul; the Lord is on thy side.
Bear patiently the cross of grief or pain.
Leave to thy God to order and provide;
In every change, He faithful will remain.
Be still, my soul; thy best, thy heavenly friend
Through thorny ways leads to a joyful end.

Be still, my soul; thy God doth undertake
To guide the future, as He has the past.
Thy hope, thy confidence let nothing shake;
All now mysterious shall be bright at last.
Be still, my soul; the waves and winds still know
His voice who ruled them while He dwelt below.

Be still, my soul; though dearest friends depart
And all is darkened in the vale of tears;
Then you will better know his love, his heart,
Who comes to soothe your sorrows and your fears.
Be still my soul, your Jesus can repay
From his own fullness all he takes away.

Be still, my soul; the hour is hastening on
When we shall be forever with the Lord.
When disappointment, grief and fear are gone,
Sorrow forgot, love's purest joys restored.
Be still, my soul; when change and tears are past
All safe and blessèd we shall meet at last.

Be still, my soul: begin the song of praise
On earth, believing, to Thy Lord on high;
Acknowledge Him in all thy words and ways,
So shall He view thee with a well-pleased eye.
Be still, my soul: the Sun of life divine
Through passing clouds shall but more brightly shine.

Katharina von Schlegel, 1752,
translated by Jane Laurie Borthwick, 1855

more encompassing picture or story."[38] From this comes a wide variety of other meanings.[39]

Having foretold the calamity of the Babylonian captivity (Isaiah 39:6-7), which was a punishment for rebellion and disobedience, Isaiah then provides his people with comfort by telling them of their certain deliverance and return from captivity as well as many other future blessings. These verses are a command to prophets and leaders to communicate this message from God so that His people will be strengthened and will not sink under their burdens. They will be able to view the catastrophe of the captivity in the light of the knowledge of their future glorious rescue.

This message of comfort was a highly charged message from Isaiah's heart to the hearts of his listeners. John Skinner (1851-1925) describes Isaiah's likely feelings as he made this prophecy:

> His state of mind borders on ecstasy; his ears are
> filled with the music of heavenly voices telling
> him that the night is far spent and the day is at
> hand; and although his home is with the exiles
> in Babylon, his gaze is fixed throughout on
> Jerusalem and the great Divine event which is the
> consummation of Israel's redemption."[40]

The same combination of God's mighty deliverance and strength-giving comfort occurs again.

> Burst into songs of joy together,
> you ruins of Jerusalem,
> for the Lord has comforted his people,
> he has redeemed Jerusalem.

(Isaiah 52:9)

It is interesting to see that comfort and joy are brought together in this verse. Jeremiah did the same when, like Isaiah, he foretold the time that God would gather His scattered people from their exile.

> I will give them comfort and joy instead of sorrow.
> (Jeremiah 31:13)

In one of the oldest Christmas carols, which has been sung in England since the sixteenth century or earlier, every verse ends with a refrain about "tidings of comfort and joy". Composed at such an early date, "comfort" no doubt still held its original dominant meaning of making strong and brave.

The source of Job's true comfort

Job's excruciating sufferings, and his agony of spirit as well as body, are recounted to us in vivid detail in the Old Testament. Before long his wife was revolted by him, most of his friends and relatives had abandoned him, his servants refused to obey him and little children were mocking him (Job 19:13-19). We will look more at this in the next chapter.

However, there were three friends who stood by him and tried, in a misguided way, to comfort him, although in fact only making his mental torment worse. But Job tells us that he did have one source of true comfort – the fact that he had not denied the words of the Holy One. (Job 6:10 ESV)

The Friend and Helper who is always with us

In most English New Testaments, occurrences of the word "comfort" are concentrated in 2 Corinthians 1, where, as we have seen, the Greek *parakalein* and words from the same root appear ten times in five verses (vv.3-7). The literal meaning of the

Greek is "to be called to the side of". The idea is of summoning someone to come and help in time of need. This root gives us the noun *parakletos* (one who is summoned to be alongside), used by Jesus to describe the Holy Spirit (John 14:16,26; 15:26; 16:7).

What kind of help does a *parakletos* give? In secular ancient Greek usage a *parakletos* could be an advisor, or an ally in battle, or someone who exhorts the troops to fight well, but the commonest meaning was a defence advocate in a court of law. Translating *parakletos* into other languages has been a great challenge because it is a word with such a depth of meaning.

A meditation on the great comfort and consolation of knowing that our faithful Friend, the Lord Jesus, walks alongside us in every season of suffering and in every trouble we encounter in this life.

Walk with me, Jesus

[1]Walk with me, Jesus,
 For dark is the night
 And hard the road.
 Jesus, walk with me.

[2]Walk with me, Jesus,
 For great is my suffering
 And endless my sorrows.
 Jesus, walk with me.

[3]Walk with me, Jesus,
 For many are my trials
 And with no respite.
 Jesus, walk with me.

[4]Walk with me, Jesus,
 For I am alone
 With none beside me.
 Jesus, walk with me.

[5]Walk with me, Jesus,
 For You are my Friend.
 Hold my hand, Jesus,
 Till my journey's end.

Patrick Sookhdeo, 2020[41]

The early Church fathers sometimes took the meaning to be "consoler" and sometimes "advocate". Some English translations, reluctant to diminish the rich variety of meanings by selecting just one of them, put "Paraclete" where Jesus speaks of the Holy Spirit. Wycliffe decided to use the word "Comforter", by which he indicated that the Holy Spirit fills us with courage and strength to cope with whatever comes our way.

The word *parakletos* was also used by John to describe Jesus Himself (1 John 2:1), but there the context shows clearly that John was employing the word in its main everyday sense at the time he lived, that is, a defence advocate in a law-court. A *parakletos* would speak to the judges on behalf of the accused, presenting their case in the most favourable light, and, as a friend of the accused, giving them a character reference. So "if anybody does sin, we have an advocate with the Father – Jesus Christ, the Righteous One." Let us remember that when Jesus spoke four times of the Holy Spirit as the *parakletos*, this was part of the meaning of that wonderful word, along with our counsellor and our consoler, our friend and ally who fights for us in the spiritual battle, and the encourager who urges us to stand firm and face our perils and difficulties with courage.

The Holy Spirit is to us all that Jesus was to His first followers. Elsewhere the Holy Spirit is called the Spirit of Jesus (Acts 16:6-7). He teaches us what Jesus taught the Twelve (John 14:26; 16:14) particularly about sin, righteousness and judgment (John 16:7-10). He guides us into all truth – Jesus called Him three times the "Spirit of truth" (John 14:17; 15:26; 16:13). He also reveals Jesus to us, who did not have the opportunity to meet our Saviour on this earth (John 15:26).

What a holy mystery it is that Jesus' going away was for our good, so that we could be sent the *parakletos*, the friend and helper to be alongside us (John 16:6-7) for ever (John 14:16).

This is how Jesus fulfils His promise to be with us always, to the very end of the age (Matthew 28:20).

The God who always comforts us in all our troubles

Let us now turn to what Paul wrote to the Corinthians about *parakalein*. It was unusual for Paul to begin a letter by pouring out his personal anguish as he does in this one. But he had just come through a time of terrible suffering and the wonderful message that he gives to the Corinthian believers is that God the Father is "the God of all comfort who comforts us in all our troubles, so that we can comfort those in any trouble with the comfort we ourselves receive from God." (2 Corinthians 1:3-4)

The God of all *parakleseos* (v.3) is the God who is always there as our *parakletos*. Paul also calls him the "Father of compassion" (v.3) so we know that tender consolation was in Paul's mind. But that was not all. For the God of all comfort is the God who does more than sympathise. He is the God who strengthens us and inspires us to endure. He is the God who encourages us to face our troubles boldly and bravely. If it is not irreverent, we might even say He is the God who cheers us on.[42]

The Trinity of Comforters

We rightly recognise that the three Persons of our Triune God have different roles. But in the matter of comforting – in its full Biblical sense – our Creator, our Saviour and our Sustainer are all active; they all take the role of *parakletos*. God the Father is the God of all comfort (2 Corinthians 1:3), God the Son is our advocate (1 John 2:1), and God the Holy Spirit is the promised Paraclete to be with us for ever (John 14:16).

Our heavenly Father always comforts for it is His nature to comfort. We can depend on His comfort for it will never fail. His comfort is abundant and overflowing (2 Corinthians 1:5). Not only does our Father always comfort, but He comforts us in all our troubles (2 Corinthians 1:4a). We may deduce also that He comforts us in any kind of trouble because we learn from Him how to do that for our brothers and sisters (2 Corinthians 1:4b).

What kind of troubles are these? Paul uses the word *thlipsis* in this passage, and later in the same letter he uses the somewhat stronger term *stenochoria*.[43] It is interesting to note the literal meaning of these words. *Thlipsis* is a crushing weight or pressure, and *stenochoria* is confinement in a small space. Both can be used to describe real physical suffering. Centuries ago English law had a punishment that consisted of placing heavy weights on a person's chest until they were crushed to death. The torture method of confining people in a box or cage so small that they can neither stand nor sit nor lie down has been used in many countries and at many times.

Metaphorically, we all know the feeling of pressure as troubles of various kinds become a burden weighing us down. We all know problems from which we feel there is no escape. Paul's words cover the whole spectrum of troubles that we may face and his message is that the God of comfort is alongside us in them all, to give us strength and courage. His comfort enables us to pass the breaking-point without breaking.

Comforting others – a circle of blessing

What's more, our own suffering can equip us to be "an agent of God's bountiful comfort",[44] a channel of God's strength and courage for others in distress. As we have already seen, Paul tells the Corinthians that God comforts us so that we can comfort others in trouble with the same comfort God has given us (2 Corinthians 1:4). Later in the letter he gives a specific example of this.

> For when we came into Macedonia, we had
> no rest, but we were harassed at every turn –
> conflicts on the outside, fears within. But God,
> who comforts the downcast, comforted us by the
> coming of Titus, and not only by his coming but
> also by the comfort you had given him.
>
> (2 Corinthians 7:5-7.)

The Corinthians comforted Titus, Titus comforted Paul – and then Paul comforted the Corinthians, making a complete circle of blessing.

> If we are distressed, it is for your comfort and
> salvation; if we are comforted, it is for your
> comfort, which produces in you patient
> endurance of the same sufferings we suffer.
>
> (2 Corinthians 1:6)

We see again in this verse the nature of Christian comfort, for the result of comforting is a change in attitude of the one comforted, not a change in their circumstances. The new attitude is neither unfounded sunny optimism nor permission to wallow in self-pity. It is a "patient endurance" that is triumphant, even joyful – it is not about holding on through gritted teeth. Nourished by a fresh infusion of divine power, we are comforted by a renewed inner experience of God's grace, our spiritual muscles strengthened and we have courage to cope.

7
The joy of the LORD

Weeping may endure for a night,
but joy comes in the morning.

(Psalm 30:5 NKJV)

This is the day that the Lord has made;
we will rejoice and be glad in it.

(Psalm 118:24 NKJV)

"The joy of the Lord is your strength." So said Nehemiah to
the exiles who had returned to rebuild Jerusalem. (Nehemiah
8:10). But the question arises: how can joy be strength? To
the logical mind this does not seem to make sense. For what
relationship can there be between joy, which indicates a blithe

gladness and delight, and strength, which indicates a tough robustness? Yet Nehemiah affirmed, in the face of numerous difficulties, that the joy *of the Lord* will be the strength of His suffering people.

As we have seen in the last chapter, troubles, hardships and afflictions are often described in the Bible as pressure (*thlipsis*) or confinement in a small cramped space (*stenochoria*). It is interesting to note that, in the Psalms, a state of joy is sometimes expressed as the relief of coming into a large space.

When we feel downcast, drained or overwhelmed it may seem hard to be either joyful or strong, let alone both. To understand the relationship between joy and strength, it is important to consider the breadth of possibilities in the word "joy" and then we discover how this certain promise of Scripture can be fulfilled in us today.

Jesus gives us joy. Joy is a key part of the Christ-like character described by the nine facets of the "fruit of the Spirit" (Galatians 5:22). Of course love, which is the pre-eminent Christian trait, heads the list. Following immediately after it is joy.[45]

Joy in our relationship with Christ

The same teaching – about love issuing in joy – was given by the Lord Jesus Himself.

> As the Father has loved me, so have I loved
> you. Now remain in my love. If you keep my
> commands, you will remain in my love, just as
> I have kept my Father's commands and remain
> in his love. I have told you this so that my
> joy may be in you and that your joy may be
> complete. My command is this: love each other
> as I have loved you. (John 15:9-12)

Speaking just hours before His death, Jesus has already promised His disciples peace (John 14:27). Now He tells them how they may also have joy – complete, full and overflowing joy. This joy comes from remaining in Jesus' love, which comes in turn from obeying His commands. In the words of the eighteenth-century English hymn-writer Joseph Swain, "Love will make obedience sweet."[46] From Jesus' words, we know that the sweetness of loving obedience includes joy - joy for us and joy for our Beloved.

Just as the peace that Jesus gives is different from any peace that the world can give, so His joy is different from the world's joy. For it is a joy that does not depend on our earthly circumstances. It is a joy that springs from our eternal relationship with Him: a relationship in which He showed His love by dying on the cross of Calvary and we delight to show our love and to bring Him joy by obeying His commands.

Marvellously and wonderfully, the whole of creation rejoices because of the Lord's righteousness and His redeeming love for us. The mountains sing together for joy, the rivers clap their hands, the trees and forests burst into song. (Psalm 98; Isaiah 44:23; 55:12)

To love and be loved in return, even in a human relationship, cannot but bring joy. How much more joy, then, to love and be loved by the High King of heaven! This is what enabled the prophet Habakkuk to declare, in the midst of calamitous famine, with total crop failure and loss of livestock, "Yet I will rejoice in the LORD, I will be joyful in God my Saviour." (Habakkuk 3:17-18)

> Jesus, the very thought of Thee
> With sweetness fills my breast;

But sweeter far Thy face to see,
And in Thy presence rest.

Jesus, our only joy be Thou,
As Thou our prize wilt be;
Jesus, be Thou our glory now
And through eternity.[47]

Joy in suffering

The Bible also teaches us other reasons for a believer
to be joyful in the most unlikely situations. Troubles and
suffering of any kind can help us grow in faith. Many people
strengthen their muscles by exercise, sometimes of the most
painful kind, choosing to push their bodies to the limits of
endurance. So it is with our spiritual strength: testing helps
us to become strong in the Lord. Therefore, James tells us,
we must view such trials and tribulations as "pure joy".

> Consider it pure joy, my brothers and
> sisters, whenever you face trials of many kinds,
> because you know that the testing of your
> faith produces perseverance. Let perseverance
> finish its work so that you may be mature and
> complete, not lacking anything.
>
> (James 1:2-4)

Perhaps if James had been living in the twenty-first
century, he might have compared the "trials of many kinds"
to various items of equipment in a gym, each one useful for
strengthening us in a different way.

The apostle Paul knew this too.

> ... we rejoice in our sufferings, knowing that
> suffering produces endurance, and endurance
> produces character, and character produces hope.
>
> (Romans 5:3-4 ESV)

Even non-Christians speak of hardship as being "character-forming" but when Christians endure difficulties the character that is being formed in us should be the character of Christ. What a gift! What a reason to rejoice!

Joy in faithfulness

Job had more earthly suffering than most. All his children died in various natural disasters, his immense wealth was lost, his good reputation in society was ruined, his health was destroyed by painful and no doubt revolting sores from head to toe, his wife turned against him and urged him to blame God, and his well-meaning but foolish friends told him to blame himself.

Job felt the full anguish of his terrible situation, completely unaware of what was going on in the heavenlies or that earthly blessings would later be restored to him. Lest we should think the saintly Job sailed through his ordeal without the agony the rest of us would have experienced, he tells us plainly that he is not made of stone or bronze – strong materials but with no feelings (Job 6:12). Job certainly did feel his suffering. Yet, in the midst of his wretchedness, he had one source of joy: his own faithfulness to the Lord. He longed for death to put an end to his suffering so that he could be sure to have kept his faith throughout his ordeal.

> I would still have this consolation – my joy in
> unrelenting pain – that I had not denied the
> words of the Holy One

> (Job 6:10)

Henry Jackson van Dyke (1852-1933), an American pastor, professor of English and at one time American ambassador to the Netherlands and Luxembourg, was guest preacher at Williams College, Williamstown, Massachusetts in 1907. While there, inspired by the beauty of the mountains, he wrote the words below, to be sung to the stirring melody "Ode to Joy" from Beethoven's ninth symphony. ("Ode to Joy" was a 1785 poem by Schiller that Beethoven incorporated in his symphony, completed in 1824.) Later van Dyke described the hymn saying, "These verses are simple expressions of common Christian feelings and desires in this present time — hymns of today that may be sung together by people who know the thought of the age, and are not afraid that any truth of science will destroy religion, or any revolution on earth overthrow the kingdom of Heaven. Therefore this is a hymn of trust and joy and hope."

The Hymn of Joy

Joyful, joyful, we adore Thee,
God of glory, Lord of love;
Hearts unfold like flowers before Thee,
Opening to the sun above;
Melt the clouds of sin and sadness,
Drive the dark of doubt away;
Giver of immortal gladness,
Fill us with the light of day!

All Thy works with joy surround Thee,
Earth and heaven reflect Thy rays,
Stars and angels sing around Thee,
Centre of unbroken praise;
Field and forest, vale and mountain,
Flowery meadow, flashing sea,
Singing bird and flowing fountain
Call us to rejoice in Thee.

Thou art giving and forgiving,
Ever blessing, ever blest,
Wellspring of the joy of living,
Ocean-depth of happy rest!
Thou our Father, Christ our Brother,
All who trust in Him are Thine;
Teach us how to love each other,
Lift us to the joy divine.

Mortals, join the happy chorus,
Which the morning stars began;
Father-love is reigning o'er us,
Brother-love binds man to man.
Ever singing, march we onward,
Victors in the midst of strife;
Joyful music lifts us Son-ward
In the triumph song of life.

Henry J. van Dyke, 1907

And this was no quiet inward rejoicing. The word translated "joy" in the NIV Bible is expressed in some translations as leaping or cavorting for joy or exulting. This great joy can be ours, too, in times of hardship, if we are faithful to our loving heavenly Father and continue to trust in His goodness.

Joy in persecution

Sometimes our suffering is not just the normal difficulties of life, but comes as a result of our faith and witness to the Lord. When suffering becomes persecution for Christ's sake, we have an extra reason to be joyful.

As the Lord Jesus told His disciples,

> Blessed are you when people insult you, persecute you and falsely say all kinds of evil against you because of me. Rejoice and be glad, because great is your reward in heaven, for in the same way they persecuted the prophets who were before you.
>
> (Matthew 5:11-12)

The first of His disciples to experience this particular blessedness ("happiness" is a better translation) were the apostles, who were arrested on the orders of the Jewish religious leaders and put in prison. An angel miraculously freed them, whereupon the temple guard promptly re-arrested them. The Sanhedrin were all set to have the obstreperous preachers put to death, but the apostles were saved again, this time by Gamaliel's intervention. Nevertheless, they were flogged, which was certainly not a light punishment if it was the traditional Jewish "forty lashes minus one".

After all this the apostles were released - and went away rejoicing. To them it was a matter of joy and celebration that they had been given the privilege of suffering for Christ.

> The apostles left the Sanhedrin, rejoicing
> because they had been counted worthy of
> suffering disgrace for the Name.
>
> (Acts 5:41)

Likewise, the newly converted Christians in Pisidian Antioch were filled with joy – and with the Holy Spirit – even after Paul and Barnabas, who had so recently brought them the Gospel, were forced out of their city by those who had been deliberately incited against them (Acts 13:50-52). The new believers in Thessalonica evidently suffered severely for their faith too (some examples are given in Acts 17:5-8), yet nothing dimmed their Spirit-given joy (1 Thessalonians 1:6).

Peter gives the same message in his first letter, which was written to Christians in situations of pressure and persecution: you are blessed when you suffer for Christ and should respond by praising God. And he adds another reason for rejoicing in such situations – we are participating in the sufferings of Christ Himself.

> Dear friends, do not be surprised at the fiery
> ordeal that has come on you to test you, as
> though something strange were happening to
> you. But rejoice inasmuch as you participate
> in the sufferings of Christ, so that you may be
> overjoyed when his glory is revealed. If you are
> insulted because of the name of Christ, you

> are blessed, for the Spirit of glory and of God
> rests on you. If you suffer, it should not be as a
> murderer or thief or any other kind of criminal,
> or even as a meddler. However, if you suffer as
> a Christian, do not be ashamed, but praise God
> that you bear that name.
>
> (1 Peter 4:12-16)

Joy in the early Church

Paul commanded the Christians of Thessalonica to be full of joy always (1 Thessalonians 5:16) and his letter to the Christians at Philippi has been called "the epistle of joy" because joy in the Lord is such a strong theme within it (e.g. Philippians 3:1; 4:4,10). The Greek verb *chairo* (usually translated as "rejoice" or "be glad") occurs 60 times[48] in the New Testament, almost half of these occurrences being in Paul's letters. In addition we find the noun *chara* (joy, delight) and the verb *synchairo* (or *sunchairo*) meaning to "rejoice together with", for rejoicing is not a solitary activity.

In addition there is a pair of words, the noun *agalliasis* and its related verb, which refer to a more exuberant and ecstatic kind of joy, sometimes translated "exultation". This extreme word is used very sparingly in the New Testament. One example is when the unborn John the Baptist leaps with a wild and exultant joy in the womb of Elizabeth as she is greeted by Mary, pregnant with the Messiah (Luke 1:44). Another occurs in the wonderful doxology at the end of the book of Jude, describing the day when we shall be presented faultless before God.

> Now unto him that is able to keep you from
> falling, and to present you faultless before the

presence of his glory with exceeding joy, to the
only wise God our Saviour, be glory and majesty,
dominion and power, both now and ever. Amen.

(Jude v24-25 KJV)

One more of these rare occurrences of *agalliasis* is in a
seemingly much more humdrum context: the description
of the fellowship of the early believers when they "broke
bread in their homes and ate together with glad and sincere
hearts" (Acts 2:46). It would be more accurate to say that
they ate together with "exulting and sincere hearts" or
"ecstatic and sincere hearts". So the home-based worship
meetings of the early believers were far from humdrum. As
they remembered their Lord in the breaking of bread and
ate together, their joy was like that of the unborn John the
Baptist rejoicing in the presence of the unborn Messiah or
like the joy we shall feel when we see God in His heavenly
glory.

We have already seen several of the main reasons for
the first Christians to rejoice, but the New Testament
gives many more. We have noted the joy of an ongoing
relationship with Christ, but there is a special joy when
that relationship begins, the joy of an individual because of
their own salvation. After his conversion and baptism the
Ethiopian eunuch went on his way rejoicing (Acts 8:39),
while the Philippian jailor was so overjoyed when he and
his family had been baptised that the rare word *agalliasis* is
used again, to show that he was absolutely bubbling over
with joy "because he had come to believe in God" (Acts
16:34). There was also joy in the early Church when others
became Christians (Acts 11:23; 15:3), when others matured
in their faith and continued in the Lord (Romans 16:19;

Colossians 2:5; 3 John v3), and when Christ was proclaimed (Philippians 1:18). They rejoiced too in the signs and wonders and mighty works of the Lord (Luke 13:17).

Joy in heaven

There is joy in heaven over each sinner who repents, joy amongst the very angels of God (Luke 15:7,10) as well as the joy of Christ (Luke 15:5) and of the Father (Luke 15:32). There is joy in heaven at the triumph of the martyrs, who overcame Satan by the blood of the Lamb, by the word of their testimony and by their own death. (Revelation 12:11-12). The saints, apostles, prophets and all heaven will rejoice when evil powers on earth, opposed to God and to His people, are at last defeated. (Revelation 18:20 ESV)

We ourselves, the ransomed and redeemed of the Lord, will be crowned with everlasting joy (Isaiah 35:9-10). We shall rejoice and be glad at the wedding supper of the Lamb (Revelation 19:7-9). And what will be our feelings when we see His face? (Revelation 22:4)

Matthew tells us that the wise men rejoiced with "exceeding great joy" (Matthew 2:10 AV) when they saw that the star they had followed so long and so far had come to rest over a certain building in Bethlehem. The Greek phrase here is remarkably emphatic, as Matthew struggles to express their excess of joy. An almost literal translation would run: "they joyed a great joy very much." But Matthew does not even attempt to describe their feelings when they entered and saw the Christ Child. Perhaps that was a joy too great, holy and mysterious to define with human words, a joy beyond all telling. Surely that is the joy we shall feel when, after our earthly journey has come to an end, we, like the wise men, at last see Jesus face to face.

Not in that poor lowly stable,
With the oxen standing by,
We shall see Him; but in heaven,
Set at God's right hand on high;[49]

Strength in joy

"The joy of the LORD is your strength," said Nehemiah to the distraught and weeping Israelites, who had been overcome with grief as they listened to God's law being read aloud and explained to them. Obediently the people calmed themselves, began to eat and drink, and to "celebrate with great joy, because they now understood the words that had been made known to them." (Nehemiah 8:10-12)

How can joy give us strength?

As we have seen, Christian joy - the joy that Jesus wants us to have - comes from the knowledge of our eternal relationship with Him. This relationship is based on the undeserved favour of God that we call "grace", that is, the love, mercy and forgiveness freely offered to us because of Christ's atoning death.

The Greek word used in the New Testament for "grace" is *charis*; the similarity to *chara*, which as we have seen above is the normal word for "joy", is no coincidence. *Charis* was originally a secular Greek word referring to the joy-giving (*chara*-giving) nature of a thing. A good wine had *charis*, a fine turn of phrase had *charis*, a splendid building had *charis*. *Charis* was primarily an aesthetic term, describing something that gave joy to those who tasted it, heard it or saw it. It also had a secondary meaning, which was ethical, so that *charis* could be used of kind, generous and helpful people. Later on, *charis* developed the further sense of being a force or power.

The New Testament writers took this secular word *charis* and added new and awe-inspiring theological dimensions to create the Biblical concept of God's grace.[50] Yet the original sense of *charis* as "joy-giving" was not lost. For it is by God's grace that we are saved, that we have the secure and loving relationship which gives us the unshakeable, unquenchable inner gladness of Christian joy. Grace gives us strength and grace gives us joy. So, by grace, the joy of the Lord is our strength.

Yes, my soul, find rest in God;
　my hope comes from him.
Truly he is my rock and my salvation;
　he is my fortress, I shall not be shaken.
My salvation and my honour depend on God;
　he is my mighty rock, my refuge.
Trust in him at all times, you people;
　pour out your hearts to him,
　for God is our refuge.

(Psalm 62:5-8)

Notes

[1] They were published the following year as a book entitled *A Lifting Up for the Downcast*. Republished in 1961 by the Banner of Truth Trust (Edinburgh and Carlisle, PA).

[2] *Hymns occasioned by the Earthquake, March 8, 1750*, 2nd edition, London: 1750.

[3] Augustine, *Confessions*, Book I, Chapter 1.

[4] John Greenleaf Whittier, *Dear Lord and Father of Mankind*, 1884.

[5] Johnson Oatman, Jr., *When Upon Life's Billows You are Tempest Tossed*, 1897.

[6] William Bridge, *A Lifting Up for the Downcast*, p.27.

[7] Andraé Crouch's song, *Soon and Very Soon, we are Going to See the King*, 1976.

[8] Wilhelmus à Brakel, *The Christian's Reasonable Service*, first published in Dutch as *De Redelijke Godsdienst* in 1700, *Vol 1: God, Man and Christ*, translated by Bartel Elshout, edited by Joel R Beeke, Grand Rapids, MI: Reformation Heritage Books, 1995.

[9] W.E. Vine, *An Expository Dictionary of New Testament Words*, Vol. 2, London: Oliphants, 1940, p.233.

[10] Amy Carmichael, *Toward Jerusalem: Poems of Faith*, first published London: SPCK, 1936; Triangle edition, 1987 © The Dohnavur Fellowship, Dohnavur, Tamil Nadu, India, p.85.

[11] Julian of Norwich (1342/3 – after 1416), quoted in *Enfolded in Love: Daily Readings with Julian of Norwich*, London: Darton, Longman & Todd, 1980 © The Julian Shrine, Norwich, UK, p.39.

[12] Patrick Sookhdeo, *With the Eye of Faith: Meditations and Prayers*, Vienna, VA, Isaac Publishing, 2020, p.39.

[13] Patrick Sookhdeo, *With the Eye of Faith*, p.40.

[14] Helen H. Lemmel, *Turn your Eyes upon Jesus*, 1918.

[15] Patrick Sookhdeo, *With the Eye of Faith*, p.41.

[16] John Newton, *Why Should I Fear the Darkest Hour*, 1771.

[17] John Newton, *Amazing Grace*, 1772, published 1779.

[18] Patrick Sookhdeo, *With the Eye of Faith*, p. 87

[19] I am greatly indebted to Matthew Henry, the Welsh Presbyterian minister and Bible scholar (1662-1714) for some of the ideas in this chapter, which are to be found in "How to Spend Every Day with God" in *The Miscellaneous Writings of the Revd. Matthew Henry*, London: John McGowan, 1838, pp.155-159.

[20] Matthew Henry, "How to Spend Every Day with God", p.155.

[21] Matthew Henry, "How to Spend Every Day with God", p.156.

[22] From the hymn *By gracious powers so wonderfully sheltered*, translated by Fred Pratt Green and Keith Clements.

[23] Amy Carmichael, *Toward Jerusalem*, pp.40-41.

[24] Patrick Sookhdeo, *With the Eye of Faith*, p.86.

[25] Matthew Henry, "How to Spend Every Day with God", p.156.

[26] Matthew Henry, "How to Spend Every Day with God", p.157.

[27] Augustus M. Toplady. It is believed that he wrote this hymn in 1763, inspired by his experience of taking shelter from a sudden thunderstorm in a fissure in the rocks of Burrington Combe, Somerset, England.

[28] William Williams, *Guide me, O Thou Great Redeemer / Guide me, O Thou Great Jehovah*, originally written in Welsh in 1745, translated by Peter Williams (1771).

[29] From Bede's commentary on the book of Revelation, written some time between 710 and 735.

[30] C.S. Lewis, *The Last Battle*, originally published 1956; Harmondsworth: Puffin Books, 1964, pp.155,165.

[31] Charles Wesley, *Jesus, Lover of my Soul*, 1740.

[32] John Bunyan, *Pilgrim's Progress*, originally published 1678; London: Samuel Bagster and Sons, 1845, p.271.

[33] For example, 2 Corinthians 2:16, 4:12.

[34] Frances J. Crosby, *Blessed Assurance*, 1873.

[35] Richard Chenevix Trench, *Synonyms of the New Testament*, 8th edition, revised, London: Macmillan and Co., 1876, p.92.

[36] Matthew Henry, "Directions for Daily Communion with God" (1712) in *The Miscellaneous Writings of the Revd. Matthew Henry*, p.165.

[37] Patrick Sookhdeo, *With the Eye of Faith*, p.178.

[38] Rabbi Julian Sinclair, "Nachamu", *The Jewish Chronicle*, 15 August 2008, https://www.thejc.com/judaism/jewish-words/nachamu-1.4503 [accessed 3 January 2021].

[39] To draw the breath forcibly, sigh, pant, groan; to have compassion or pity (have compassion (*nachamu*) on your servants Psalm 90:13); to comfort or console oneself (Judah was comforted (*nachamu*) Genesis 38:12, NKJV); to relent, repent or change one's mind (I regret (*nachamu*) that I made them Genesis 6:7; I am weary of relenting (*nachamu*) Jeremiah 15:6, ESV); to take vengeance (I will rid Myself (*nachamu*) of My adversaries, and take vengeance on My enemies Isaiah 1:24, NKJV). What links them all is deep emotion and the obtaining of relief, whether by repentance, vengeance, or consolation.

[40] J. Skinner, *The Book of the Prophet Isaiah Chapters XL-LXVI*, Revised Version with Introduction and Notes, published as part of *The Cambridge Bible for Schools and Colleges*, Cambridge: Cambridge University Press, 1906, p.251.

[41] Patrick Sookhdeo, *With the Eye of Faith*, p.51.

[42] There is another word in New Testament Greek, *paramuthia*, which means the tender, calming consolation that is nowadays the normal meaning of "comfort" in English. *Paramuthia* and other words from the same root appear in John 11:19,31; 1 Corinthians 14:3; Philippians 2:1; 1 Thessalonians 2:12; 5:14. Sometimes the two words occur together, for example, in Philippians 2:1 which says "If you have any *paraklesos* from being united with Christ, any *paramuthia* from his love…" In 1 Thessalonians 5:14, Paul urges (*paraklesos*) his Christian brothers and sisters at Thessalonica to do several things including encourage (*paramuthia*) the disheartened.

[43] *Stenochoria* occurs only four times in the New Testament, always in conjunction with thlipsis or a word from the same root as thlipsis: Romans 2:9 trouble (*thlipsis*) and distress (*stenochoria*); Romans 8:35 trouble (*thlipsis*) or hardship (*stenochoria*); 2 Corinthians 4:8 hard pressed (*thlibomenoi*) on every side, but not crushed (*stenochoria*); 2 Corinthians 6:4 troubles (*thlipsis*), hardships and distresses (*stenochoria*).

[44] Murray J. Harris, *The Second Epistle to the Corinthians: A Commentary of the Greek Text*, Grand Rapids: Eerdmans and Milton Keynes: Paternoster, 2005, p.137.

[45] Joy, unlike most of the other aspects of the fruit of the Spirit, has the potential to be mis-used. For example, the chief priests rejoiced when Judas came to them to betray Jesus (Mark 14:11). Paul is careful to warn the Corinthian Christians that love does not rejoice at wrong-doing and injustice. Nor, we could add, does it gloat with *Schadenfreude* over other's misfortunes.

[46] Joseph Swain, *Come Ye Souls by Sin Afflicted*, 1792.

[47]Two verses from *Jesus the Very Thought of Thee*, a hymn attributed to Bernard of Clairvaux (c. 1090-1153), translated by Edward Caswall (1814-78).

[48]This figure excludes the twelve times when it is used as a form of greeting rather than in its basic sense of "rejoice".

[49]Cecil Frances Alexander, *Once in Royal David's City*, 1848.

[50]"Greek words taken up into Christian use are glorified and transformed, seeming to have waited for this adoption of them, to come to their full rights, and to reveal all the depth and the riches of the meaning which they contained, or might be made to contain." (Richard Chenevix Trench, *Synonyms of the New Testament*, p.160).

Index of
Bible references

Index

Barnabas Fund

Dr Patrick Sookhdeo is the International Director of Barnabas Fund, an interdenominational charity which provides practical help for needy Christians living in contexts of pressure and persecution.

For further information:

barnabasfund.org

UK office
9 Priory Row
Coventry
CV1 5EX
Telephone 024 7623 1923
Email info@barnabasfund.org